WRITE YOUR OWN BOOK

MYSTERY

A KID'S STEP-BY-STEP GUIDE TO CREATIVE MYSTERY WRITING

OLLIE OOD • ILLUSTRATIONS BY ALEJANDRO MIRANDA

ISBN: Paperback 978-1-990828-61-4

CalamariTales.com

Contents

Write Your Own Book–Mystery Workbook *Step-by-Step Creative Writing Prompts for Kids*

Used on its own or as a companion to *Write Your Own Book–Mystery*, this workbook is packed full of exercises and writing prompts to help you develop and finish a mystery novel. Available on Amazon.

MY NOVEL: *A Book of Blank Pages to Hold a Masterpiece of Literature*

If you need a blank book to write your novel in, check out ***My Novel***. It's got 120 lined pages, plus an appendix of worksheets to help you develop your story. Available on Amazon.

FREE DOWNLOAD!

If you need extra copies of some of the worksheets found in this book, go to **CalamariTales.com/novel-worksheets** to download your free pdf.

CalamariTales.com

Introduction

HAVE YOU EVER looked across your classroom and noticed two kids whispering to each other? I bet it intrigued you. What are they talking about? Why the big secret? Few things draw us in as much as a good mystery! Our brains love a tricky problem to figure out, a puzzle to solve, a criminal to catch.

Mysteries are so appealing to readers that almost all novels or movies have some element of a "mystery" to them. Think about it. If you've watched *Star Wars*, I bet you wondered just who Luke's father really is. In *Harry Potter*, you probably longed to know more about why Harry is "the boy who lived," and just what the deal is with Voldemort. Mysteries pull us into the story!

At its heart, a mystery involves hidden information and something to figure out. It makes us curious and interested. Just like you wonder what those two kids in class are whispering about, mystery in stories intrigues us and makes us keep reading way past our bedtime because we can't wait to learn the secrets of the story!

While most novels have some mystery to them as the story slowly unfolds, mystery stories put the intrigue centre stage. In a mystery, the point of the story is to find out who did it (the crime, murder, etc.)! We even call these kinds of stories "whodunnits."

Even though there are special qualities to a mystery novel, any experience you have with writing stories, whether novels or short stories, will be helpful. A mystery novel is first and foremost a novel before everything else. What do I mean by that? I mean your book will need, like all novels, a unique idea, interesting characters who are relatable, and a plot that hooks your readers and carries them for the entirety of the book. It is helpful if you understand a little about writing stories before diving into this book, but if not, no worries, you can still get a lot from it. If you would like to learn more about basic storytelling, we suggest you pick up the book *How to Write a Novel Before You Turn 13*.

In this book, we will focus on how you write a *mystery* novel. The book will guide you through the steps you need to create a mystery story with engaging characters, an intriguing plot, compelling clues, and red herrings (otherwise known as false clues) to throw your readers off the scent.

Writing a mystery novel may feel like a mystery in and of itself. Just how do those authors create such complicated stories? Let's shed some light on that process by getting a sneak peek at the 11 steps you will use to create a mystery book of your very own.

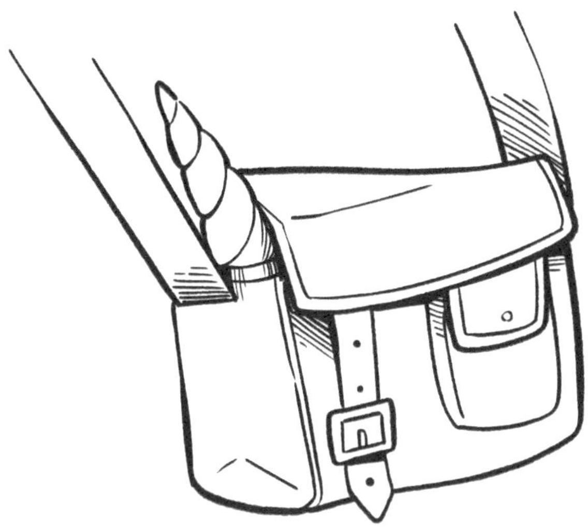

Answer These 3 Questions

These questions are:

1) **What's the crime?**

2) **Who's the villain?**

3) **Why was the crime committed?**

Your whole story will follow the journey to answer these three questions.

Write a Short Summary of your Story

Creating a short, one-page version of your entire story will help you discover what your story is, and stay on track as you write your novel. This will become the roadmap to guide your story. You may be thinking, "But I don't even know what happens in my story yet!" That's okay! Creating this super short version will actually help you get to know your story. As you write it, you'll try out different ideas. The good news is, if something doesn't seem right, you only wrote a page and can easily change it. This story summary can also grow and change as you go through the steps. Nothing is set in stone!

Create Character Profiles

As you decide *what* will happen in your story, you will naturally find yourself asking *who* this story is about. You'll villains, heros, and any other people that are necessary to the story. By creating a character profile for each of your characters, you will get to know them and watch them take shape right in front of you. It's awesome to watch them come alive!

Decide on Locations and Settings

Every story takes place in a particular time and place, and sometimes in several places. You will listen to your story to find its perfect setting. Should it take place in late 1800s London, or contemporary Dayton, Ohio? Only you and your story know the answer and this step will help you uncover it.

Choose the Point of View

Choosing the right point of view (POV) is crucial for your mystery novel. Will you dive into the intimate world of First Person, where readers see and feel everything through the eyes of your detective? Or will you opt for Third Person Limited, where an outside narrator follows just one character? Perhaps Third Person Omniscient suits your story better, offering a god-like perspective over all characters and events. Each POV brings unique strengths and challenges, shaping how your readers experience the twists and turns of your mystery.

Plot the Story

Think of your plot as the skeleton of your mystery novel; it holds everything together and gives shape to your story. A mystery needs to keep readers engaged and guessing, so include twists and turns that keep the suspense high. This outline will serve as your guide, helping you stay on track as you write, and ensuring that your story flows logically from start to finish. Don't worry if you don't have every detail figured out yet—your plot can evolve as you write. The important thing is to have a roadmap that guides you through the journey of your mystery novel.

Plan the Villain's Timeline

A mystery novel is like an old clock. On the outside, a clock looks simple—12 numbers, 2 hands. But inside, there are gears and gizmos and all the complicated machinery that keep it running. You are now the "clockmaker" of your story, and in this step, you will work out every detail of your villain's crimes and movements. This work, like the workings of a clock, won't be visible to your readers, but the effects of your planning will produce a quality mystery story.

Plan the Hero's Timeline

Just like your villain gets a special planning session, so does your hero. You will create a timeline for your hero and your villain, with your hero ever hot on the heels to catching the crook, and the villain always just one step ahead. How will the hero catch them? That's for you to plan and keep secret from your readers until the right moment.

Bury the Clues and Plant the Red Herrings

Once you've plotted your story, you will go back and plant clues along the way for your hero, (and readers) to find. Ever wonder how your favourite mystery authors are able to create such amazing clues that you didn't even notice the first time around? They know where the story is going and lay subtle clues to help the hero and readers get there. You can do it too.

But you can't make it too easy!. That isn't any fun at all! So, how do you make sure your hero and readers don't solve things too soon or too easily? Red Herrings! These false clues lead to dead-ends and force your hero to work harder to solve the case.

Unravel the Mystery

Now comes the moment everyone has been waiting for—the big reveal! After leading your hero (and readers) through twists, turns, and clever distractions, it's time to pull back the curtain and expose the truth. How will your hero piece together the clues and outsmart the villain? This is your chance to show off your storytelling skills and deliver a surprise that will leave your readers gasping! The key to a great reveal is making it both unexpected and satisfying, tying up all the loose ends in a way that makes perfect sense once the secret is out.

Write, Revise, and Refine

Once you have all your planning in place, you're ready to write! The good news is, with so much work on the front-end, you'll know where you're going and what needs to happen in each part of your book. But don't think you're done once your manuscript is complete—that's just your first draft! Revising and polishing a first draft is what turns it into a compelling and well-crafted mystery novel. This is what separates the great stories from the not-so great ones.

STEP 1

Answer These 3 Questions

1

What's the crime?

2

Who's the villain?

3

Why was the crime committed?

These three questions are the foundation of your mystery. Everything your hero discovers, every twist you throw in, and every clue you plant will revolve around answering these questions.

STEP 1

Answer These 3 Questions

Riddle Me This

THE FOUNDATION of any mystery begins with three crucial questions: What's the crime? Who's the villain? And why was the crime committed? Answering these questions is your first—and perhaps most important—task. They're not just a starting point; they are the spine of your entire story. Every twist, every clue, and every red herring will trace back to the answers you decide on right now.

Why is it so important? Because these questions give your story direction and purpose. Knowing who the villain is helps you understand the driving force behind the events that unfold. Identifying the crime gives you the central problem that your characters—and your readers—will be trying to solve. And understanding the motivation behind the crime adds depth to your story, turning a simple whodunit into a compelling narrative that keeps readers hooked.

These answers will serve as your guiding light throughout the writing process. They'll help you plot your story, develop your characters, and plant the clues that will eventually lead to the big reveal. By nailing down these details from the start, you set yourself up for success, ensuring that your mystery has a solid core that will hold everything together.

So, don't rush through this step—take the time to really think about your answers . Dive into your villain's backstory, the crime they've committed, and the motives behind their mischief. The clearer you get on these details, the stronger your mystery will be, and the more rewarding it'll feel for your readers when they finally piece it all together. After all, a well-crafted mystery is like a perfectly laid trap—irresistible and impossible to escape!

TIP

Ready to crack the case? Think of each answer as a clue that helps you unlock the mystery. Dive deep and get creative with your answers; the more detailed and surprising your answers, the richer your story will be. Consider this your detective work: the better your answers, the better your mystery.

Now that you've cracked the case of the three key questions, it's time to dig deeper into the world of mysteries. Mysteries aren't just one-size-fits-all—there are all kinds, from classic whodunits to cozy capers. The kind of mystery you choose will set the stage for your entire story, from the mood and locations to the characters who bring it to life. In the next section, we'll investigate the different sub-genres of mystery, helping you decide which twisty path your story will take. Whether you're cooking up a nail-biting thriller or a more light-hearted escapade, knowing your mystery type will keep you on the right track—or at least prevent you from barking up the wrong tree!

What's a Mystery?

Most of us can think of a few mystery stories we've read or watched, or maybe name a detective like Sherlock Holmes or Nancy Drew. But did you know there are different *kinds* of mysteries? A mystery is one kind of story, or genre, but within the genre of "mystery," there are several sub-genres. Just like the group "trees" has several sub-groups or various kinds of trees within it (apple trees, pine trees, maple trees), each kind (or genre) of story (mystery, fantasy, action/adventure) has their own sub-genres. So, before you can write your mystery, you need to know what *kind* of mystery you want to write. It can sound complicated, but really, it's not. The next few pages list the best-known sub-genres of mystery books.

Noir

This genre of mystery started in the 1930s and 40s. If you have a down-on-his-luck detective, lots of shadowy side streets, and characters smoking cigarettes leaning against lampposts in the rain, you probably have a noir. The main character, the jaded detective, is a complicated character. Who is bad? who is good? what is right? what is wrong? These ideas are less clear in noir. The story often starts when a beautiful woman comes to the detective because she is in some kind of mysterious trouble that she can't say too much about. Possibly she is being followed. This genre is very serious, brooding, and shadowy. Who knows who can be trusted? Probably not many people if you ask our world-weary and cynical detective who has seen it all. In a noir story, most of the action happens at night and in the city. Bonus points if there is fog or a scene on the docks. This can be a really fun genre to try out.

What would noir look like if you had a kid detective? Would your detective be a kid who has "seen it all?" Maybe they used to be part of the popular kids' group until they were booted out and now, they don't really fit anywhere. Maybe they have discovered a janitorial closet in the dank dark basement and have set up an office to solve school mysteries. And who says you can't turn some of the genre conventions, or norms, on their head! Noir doesn't have to just be serious. It is such a well known subgenre and is often spoofed. Maybe your detective isn't "world weary" at all. They could just be a regular kid who falls into the shadowy, and comical, underground world of middle school life. The possibilities are endless!

Cozy

Often set in a small, tight-knit community where everyone is quite an eccentric (and a suspect!), cozy mysteries are full of charm, sometimes humour, and very little gross stuff like blood, violence, or darker themes. The victim is often someone we don't know or like very much, such as a mean teacher, rich snobby lady, etc. The detective in these stories is an amateur detective, like Nancy Drew. These amateur sleuths are not professional private eyes or police but just regular people like you and me. They are also, typically, someone who likes mysteries or has a knack for noticing things and solving puzzles. Part of the fun is watching them sometimes bumble and stumble their way into solving the crime. The danger of writing a cozy mystery is your fans may hound you to write another one, and quickly!

What if you re-imagined cozy mysteries with a unique twist? Instead of a typical small town, picture the story set in an eccentric apartment building where each resident has their own quirky personality and potential motives. The amateur detective could be a curious teenager who stumbles upon secrets while helping the elderly tenants with their groceries. Imagine a story where a mysterious disappearance involves a diamond necklace, and our teenage sleuth has to navigate the building's oddball community to uncover the truth. Or consider setting a cozy mystery in a summer camp, where a young camp counsellor has to solve the mystery of the missing camp mascot while dealing with campfire stories and pranks. The key elements of charm, humour, and light-hearted suspense remain, but the setting and characters add a fresh, modern twist to the beloved cozy genre.

Police Procedural

This kind of mystery is exactly like it sounds—a police story. These stories are very realistic and carefully researched. We follow the police, usually a detective or small team, as they solve a crime, often a murder or kidnapping. They don't shy away from gritty details and real-world issues. Modern scientific crime-solving methods are put on display here, such as autopsy reports, handling of evidence with forensic science, and all the tools at their disposal. For sure there is a lot of coffee drinking, discussions at police headquarters, dead ends, and new leads. The police interview people, comb through the scene of the crime, and sometimes chase and catch suspects. If you want to write a police procedural, don't be discouraged just because you aren't a badge-carrying member of your local law-enforcement. You can research. Read books, search reputable internet sites, and maybe even interview some local police about how exactly they catch the criminals.

If you want to put a creative spin on the police procedural, set the story in a high school, with the school's hall monitors playing the roles of detectives. Instead of solving murders or kidnappings, they could investigate school-related mysteries such as stolen exam papers, vandalised lockers, or missing mascots. The security team could use their own "forensic" methods, like analysing security camera footage or tracking down clues through social media. By re-imagining the traditional police procedural in a school setting, you can retain the essence of meticulous investigation and gritty details while making it relatable for your readers.

Private Eye

Perhaps the most famous of all private eyes is Sherlock Holmes. Why is he "private?" Because this detective, for various reasons (usually his or her eccentricity), works for themself. They are so brilliant the police go to them for help! Often, the police are a bit bumbling, but our genius detective agrees to help them. Sometimes, there is even a feud with the official law enforcement, as they refuse to listen to the detective. A key feature of this subgenre is that the investigator is really the focus of the book. Sure, there is a crime, usually a murder, and we want to find out who did it and why, but we love following along with this private eye and seeing how they will catch the crook this time. Sometimes the detective is highly intelligent, complete with personality quirks. But even if they are just an average person thrown into the detective role, we never doubt they have a good heart and ultimately want justice done. This leads them to continue solving crimes.

Imagine a middle school student who has a knack for solving puzzles. This nerdy student, known for their intelligence and curiosity, starts investigating mysteries when their classmates come to them for help with missing items, mysterious notes, or strange happenings around the school. The local police, portrayed as a bit bumbling and dismissive of the kids' concerns, refuse to accept the young detective's assistance. This student sleuth uses their problem-solving skills and keen observation to crack cases, all while juggling homework, friendships, and after-school activities.

Locked Room

Have you ever been stuck in a car with your family for hours on end? It definitely brings out conflict doesn't it! In a locked room mystery, the characters are forced together for the entirety of the story, and just like with your family on vacation, the good and bad parts of everyone come out. Interesting characters with interesting relationships are a big part of these stories. For some reason, like a theft or a storm, no one can leave. The setting plays a key element here, with the story unfolding throughout many rooms but all in the limited location. Large manor houses with guests for a weekend party is perfect for this sub-genre. If you've ever played Clue, this is the idea. Sometimes outside characters come in, such as a detective, but it is limited.

Why not turn the locked-room mystery into an exciting adventure for kids by setting it in a school during a weekend club meeting? A small group of students and a teacher advisor stuck in the school building due to a sudden snowstorm. Strange things start happening: the class president's year-end project goes missing, cryptic messages appear on the chalkboards, and the school's prized trophy is taken from its display case. With no one allowed to leave the building until the storm clears, the kids must work together to solve the mystery. Each student has a unique personality and skill, from the tech-savvy kid who hacks into the school's security system to the artist who sketches out possible suspects and scenarios. The teacher advisor, trying to keep everyone calm and organised, ends up being just as much a part of the mystery, with their own secrets and quirks coming to light.

Whatever kind of mystery you decide on, it still needs to be a good story. How do you write a good story, you ask? Well, that's the big question, isn't it! Here's the short answer:

Create Interesting Characters

Your characters, especially your main character, will make or break your story. Figure out who they are and what makes them tick. What do they want? What do they fear? Yes, think about what they look like and what they wear, but this is less important. Your readers don't care if your detective has brown hair. They do care why your detective is afraid of heights, or why they get sad every time they look at a picture of a certain little girl. Maybe she's the girl they failed to help? See what I mean! That is SO much more interesting than the fact they have a plaid jacket. Give your characters hurts and hopes and a history that made them who they are today.

Make Things Happen!

Writing isn't a story if nothing happens. The things that happen and how people act and react to those things is what we call the "plot." That's what makes a story! Luckily, you're writing a mystery, so you already know what will happen in your book: some crime will occur and it will be solved. But remember as you write, keep things happening, new info unfolding, and your characters and readers guessing what will come next.

Use Language to Show the Story

Use sensory details, such as taste, touch, sight, sound, smell, to put your readers in the scene. Think about how your characters feel, and show that to your readers. Don't say "Hank was angry there were no new leads," show Hank slamming his coffee cup down and muttering "No new leads, again."

Build a Solid Story Structure

Good stories often have a certain shape to them. Think about it. Even though people come in all shapes and sizes, there are certain things that remain the same and seem right: The torso is about 1/3 of the body height, the legs 2/3. Your foot is as long as your elbow to your wrist. The same goes with stories. Stories usually have a beginning, a middle, and an end. And, in this structure, the middle is about 1/2 of the story, with the beginning and ending each taking roughly 1/4. Certain events tend to happen in the beginning of stories, and different ones in the end. Stories have a shape, and part of your job as the author is to shape your story into the best version of itself.

One last thing, as you write your story, remember your readers deserve to be treated fairly. That means you don't lead them along one path, then suddenly spring a totally different ending that comes out of nowhere. You must plant clues along the way and allow your readers a chance to solve the puzzle.

STEP 2

Write a Short Summary of Your Story

Don't worry about getting it perfect—just get it down! Writing a brief summary helps you see the big picture. It's like a roadmap for your mystery, guiding you as you write. Take a deep breath and start summarising; this will be one of the most helpful tools you can have as you plot your story.

STEP 2

Write a Short Summary of Your Story

Finding Your Story Idea

COMING UP WITH A STORY idea can be one of the most exciting parts of writing a mystery novel. Your idea is the seed that will grow into a full-fledged story, and it all starts with a simple concept. How do you come up with that perfect idea? Here are some tips and examples to help you get started.

Start by thinking about what you enjoy. Do you love stories about secret passages, hidden treasures, or schoolyard sleuths? Your interests can be a great source of inspiration. For example, if you love animals, maybe your story is about a kid detective who solves mysteries at the local zoo.

Another way to generate ideas is to ask "What if?" questions. What if your detective finds a hidden diary that leads to a treasure hunt? What if the school science fair project goes missing just before the big day? "What if" questions help you imagine different scenarios and spark your creativity.

Remember, just like anything, it takes practice to be creative and use your imagination. But you can do it! I suggest you get a notebook and keep it by your bed. Every day, try to write whatever pops into your head for five minutes straight. Don't stop writing until the five minutes are up.

You can also write down your dreams when you first wake up, or take your notebook in the car and stare out the window as you drive around town. What do you notice? What do you wonder about? Write down anything that seems interesting to you. Describe quirky and unusual people you see. Write about crimes that someone might commit (after all, you *are* writing a mystery book). The point is give yourself time and space to be creative and the ideas will come.

You can also draw inspiration from real life. Think about curious or mysterious things that have happened to you or someone you know. Maybe you read about a strange event in the news that could be turned into a captivating mystery. Real-life experiences can provide a solid foundation for your story.

Why Write a Short Summary?

Once you have your story idea, it's a good idea to write a short summary of your story. This is sometimes called a "story blueprint." A summary is a brief version of your entire story that helps you understand the main plot and stay on track as you write. Here's why it's important:

Focus and Clarity

Writing a summary forces you to think about the main elements of your story. Who is your detective? What is the main mystery they need to solve? Why is the crime committed? By answering these questions in your summary, you can clarify your story idea and ensure it makes sense. For example, your summary idea might be: "A seventh-grader named Alex discovers a series of coded messages hidden around the school. With the help of his friends, he must decode the messages to uncover a plot to sabotage the school play."

Roadmap for Writing

A summary acts as a roadmap for your writing journey. It outlines the major events and turning points in your story, helping you see the big picture. This way, when you sit down to write, you know where your story is headed and what you need to include. Your summary might start with, "Alex finds the first coded message in his locker," and end with, "Alex and his friends uncover the villain's plan just in time to save the play."

Flexibility and Growth

Your summary is not set in stone. It's a living document that can change and grow as your story develops. If you come up with a better idea or realise something isn't working, you can update your summary. This flexibility allows you to experiment and improve your story without getting lost in the details.

Example of a Short Summary

During the school's annual music concert, a priceless antique violin goes missing from the music room. Twelve-year-old Jordan, an enthusiastic member of the school's orchestra, is determined to find out who stole it. With the help of his friend, Ava, Jordan begins to piece together the clues. They start by interviewing fellow students, teachers, and anyone who had access to the music room.

As they dig into the case, they uncover a series of puzzling details, including a broken lock and a suspiciously quiet janitor. Jordan and Ava discover that the violin was stolen to sabotage the performance of a talented student who was the concert's star performer. The thief, a rival musician hoping to steal the spotlight, planned to frame someone else for the crime. With their sharp detective work, Jordan and Ava recover the stolen violin and expose the true culprit, ensuring the concert goes on as planned."

This summary gives a clear picture of the main plot, characters, and setting, providing a strong foundation to build the story.

By coming up with a solid story idea and crafting a short summary, you'll have a clear blueprint to guide your writing. This will help you stay focused and organised, making the process of writing your mystery novel both fun and manageable.

TIP

Keep your summary focused and simple! Think of it as a sneak peek into your story—a quick, exciting preview that captures the essence of your mystery. This will be your guiding light as you dive deeper into writing your book.

STEP 3

Create Character Profiles

As you decide *what* will happen in your story, you will naturally find yourself asking *who* this story is about. Your characters are about to come to life! Jot down their quirks, secrets, and strengths. By the time you finish, you'll know your heroes and villains like old friends. This is where your story starts to get personal, so have fun with it!

STEP 3

Create Character Profiles

Heroes, Villains, & Everyone Else

WHEN YOU THINK about a mystery story, two characters probably leap out right away. No, I'm not talking about Sherlock Holmes and Dr Watson, although that is half right. I'm talking more about character types, which means kinds of characters that show up in stories over and over. For a mystery, there are two characters you absolutely need above all else—the detective and the villain.

The Hero

Let's look first at the protagonist, also known as the hero. In a mystery, your protagonist is the detective, but what kind of detective will they be? If you are writing a cozy mystery, your detective might be a student helper in the library, maybe even a mystery book fan, who is thrown into the role of detective by accident. If you are writing a police procedural, the detective will be a cop, or maybe the child of a cop if you want a kid protagonist. What kind of detective you have all depends on which sub-genre of mystery you are writing and for which age group.

To create a fascinating detective character, you need to answer a few questions. Who is your detective? Why are they involved in solving the crime? What is their reason or motive for getting involved? Lastly, what kinds of qualities does your detective have that will help them solve the crime? You might also ask what your detective cares about and what they fear? If your detective has to face things they fear as they solve the crime, so much the better!

You should also think about what your detective looks like, but even better, does your detective have any particular quirks or unusual habits? Are they very particular and tidy or a total slob? What details can show these qualities in your story? As you create your detective, remember these common qualities for mystery story main characters as well: a special ability to notice details, an above average sense of curiosity, and an inability to stay out of trouble.

The Villain

Of course, no mystery story is complete with just a detective. Cue the dramatic music—we need a baddy! Somebody has to commit the crime for your detective to solve, right? Having a good villain is just as important as having a good detective!

When creating villains, you have some options. A villain can be a truly evil mastermind like Dr Moriarty (Sherlock Holmes's main enemy), or your villain can be a person who accidentally committed a crime. Another option is a villain who is normally a good person but committed a crime out of self-defense. There are many kinds of villains to create! Just remember, your villain, like your detective, needs a strong motive to go into the world of crime and act as they do. They must be believable and their actions must make sense. For example, you may think a sweet old lady would make a great villain, and you're right! But if that sweet old lady doesn't have a believable reason to commit her crime, no one will believe it. Even being "evil" isn't enough of a reason. What does your evil villain have to gain by their actions? Asking these "why" questions, such as "why would they do that?" is a good way to get started.

It may be helpful to ask why your villain is evil to begin with. Were they born bad, or did something sad or terrible happen to them? How did they become who they are today?

The characters are the heartbeat that drives the plot forward. From clever detectives to cunning villains, each character plays a unique role in unravelling the mystery. While there are countless character types you could include in your story, here are some common ones you'll want to think about as you build your cast.

The Victim

The victim is the focal point of the crime, whether they are murdered, kidnapped, stolen from, or otherwise harmed. Their backstory, relationships, and circumstances are essential as they provide context and motive for the crime. Understanding the victim's life and how it intersects with other characters can enrich the mystery and drive the plot.

The Client

The person who hires or asks the detective to solve the case. They often have a personal stake in the mystery being resolved.

The Sidekick

Don't forget sidekicks as well. Most detectives have somebody who they brainstorm with and confide in as they solve the crime. Having a sidekick is important because it allows us to see into the detective's mind and follow along as they solve the crime.

Witnesses & Persons of Interest

Witnesses and persons of interest play crucial roles in advancing the investigation. Witnesses are individuals who have seen or heard something significant related to the crime, while persons of interest might have connections to the case or possess relevant information. Their testimonies and interactions with the detective help unravel the mystery and provide essential clues.

The Authority Figure

This character could be a police officer, a chief inspector, or a judge who is involved in the investigation. They might work with or against the main detective, depending on the story.

The Expert

The expert character could be a forensic scientist, a historian, or a criminal profiler that has specialised knowledge that is crucial to solving the mystery.

The Suspects

Perhaps the most important of all the side characters is your list of suspects! These are characters who are potential villains, each with their own motive, means, and opportunity to commit the crime. These characters make your story interesting and keep your readers guessing "whodunnit."

The Antagonist

Another important character in a mystery novel is the antagonist. They may or may not be the villain. This character gets in the way of your detective as they try to solve the crime. This could be a rival investigator, an overbearing authority figure, or even a well-meaning friend who inadvertently hinders progress. Even a bungling, but well meaning, sidekick could act as an antagonist sometimes!

The Problem Character

This might be the best friend who always has relationship problems and needs to talk (at just the wrong time), or the neighbour who shows up at the wrong place and gets kidnapped. These characters also act as antagonists as the detective must continually help and bail them out of trouble, and divert attention away from the case.

The Reporter

This person may be an actual news reporter, or just a nosey character who gets into everyone's business and isn't afraid to share what they know. These characters are helpful in your story as they tell secrets and help your detective figure out potential motives of suspects.

Whatever characters you create, always do your best to make them realistic with unique characteristics. Can you give the person some unusual interest or hobby? What about a strange mannerism or habit? If you have trouble coming up with ideas, go sit somewhere in a crowded place with a notebook. What are things you notice about the people that walk by? What do they look like? How do they talk? Do they have any qualities that stand out, like being very tall, or very short? There is no law against stealing ideas from the real people you come into contact with every day. Become a detective of details and figure out just the right one to make your characters come alive (even if just for a few pages before they are murdered or kidnapped!)

Use the next few pages to help you create character sketches for all your characters. (You'll need extra paper to create one for each of the characters in your story.) A character sketch is like a mini-dossier that helps you figure out what your characters look like, how they act, and what makes them tick. Answering these questions for each of your characters will help you explore and define your characters so they feel real and exciting. The more you know about your characters, the more vivid and realistic they will become in your story!

Remember, the characters in a book keep readers captivated, or bore them into turning on the TV. Don't skimp on creating your characters! Put in the work and you'll be surprised at the interesting people who pop into your story.

TIP

Get to know your characters like they're your best friends—or your worst enemies! The more you understand their quirks, motivations, and secrets, the more they'll come alive on the page. A well-rounded character can make your mystery truly unforgettable.

The Basics

Name:

Age:

Gender:

Occupation/Role *(student, parent, teacher, etc.)*:

Physical Appearance *(height, build, hair colour, eye colour, etc.)*:

Any special features *(a scar, odd hair, a limp, etc.)*:

Style *(clothing, accessories, any notable fashion choices)*:

Voice *(accent, tone, pitch, unique speech patterns)*:

Mannerisms *(common facial expressions, how they walk, move, etc.)*:

The Backstory

Background *(Where are they from? home life, significant life events)*:

Motivations *(What drives them? What are their goals and desires?)*:

Fears and Insecurities *(What are they afraid of? What weaknesses do they try to hide?)*:

Key Relationships *(Family, friends, enemies, mentors—how do these relationships shape them?)*:

Past Experiences *(Significant moments that shaped their personality or worldview)*:

Did anything bad happen to the character that formed who they are today?

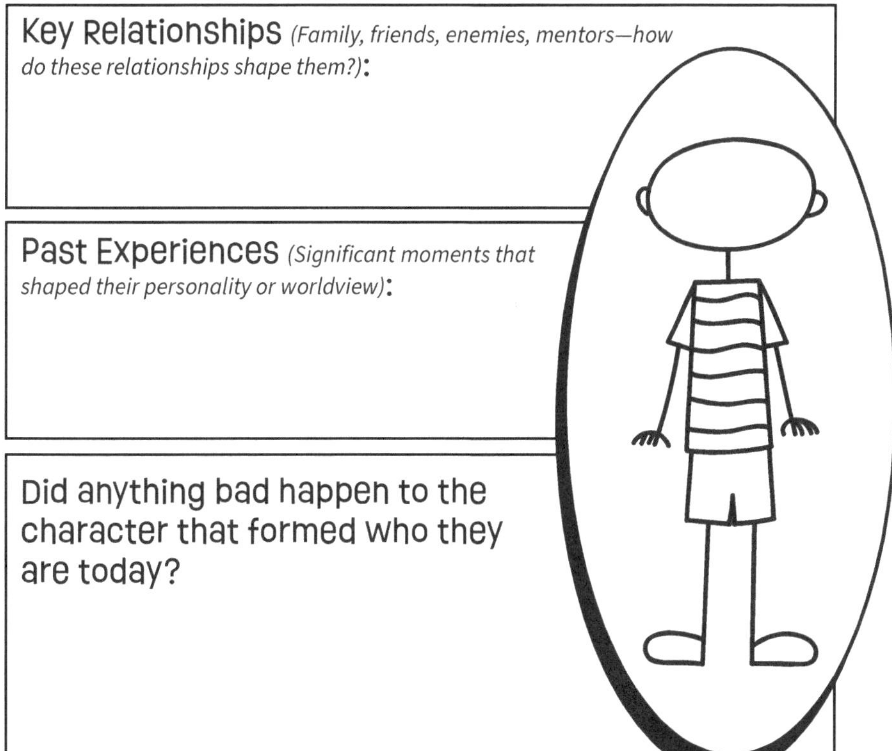

Personality

Core Traits *(Describe their personality traits —optimistic, cynical, ambitious, etc)*:

Habits and Quirks *(Any unique habits, or quirky behaviours)*:

Strengths *(What are they particularly good at?)*:

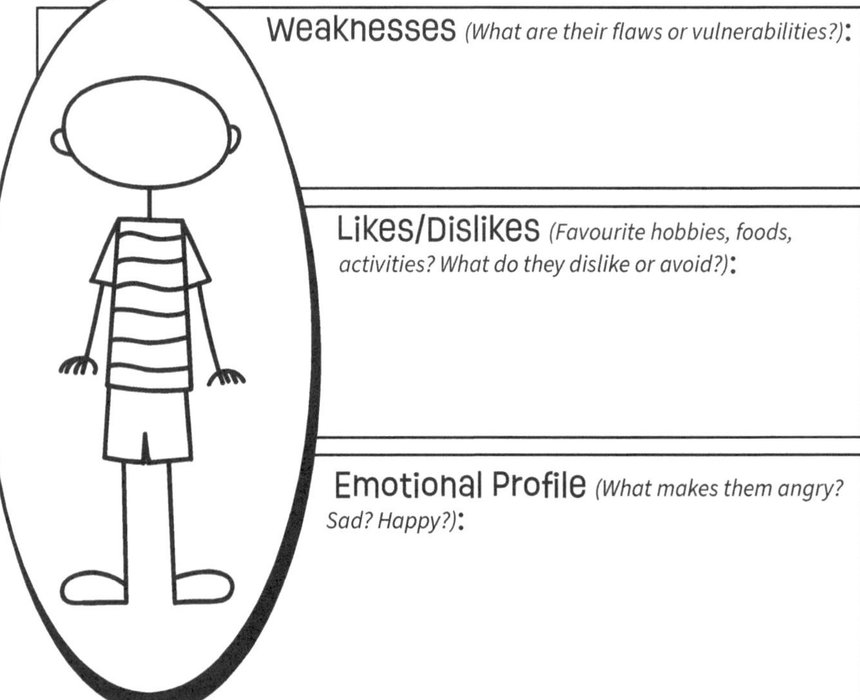

Weaknesses *(What are their flaws or vulnerabilities?)*:

Likes/Dislikes *(Favourite hobbies, foods, activities? What do they dislike or avoid?)*:

Emotional Profile *(What makes them angry? Sad? Happy?)*:

Role in the Story

Role *(Hero, villain, sidekick, mentor—what part do they play in the story?)*:

Character Arc *(How does this character change from the beginning to the end of the story?)*:

Relationships in Story *(How do they interact with the other characters?)*:

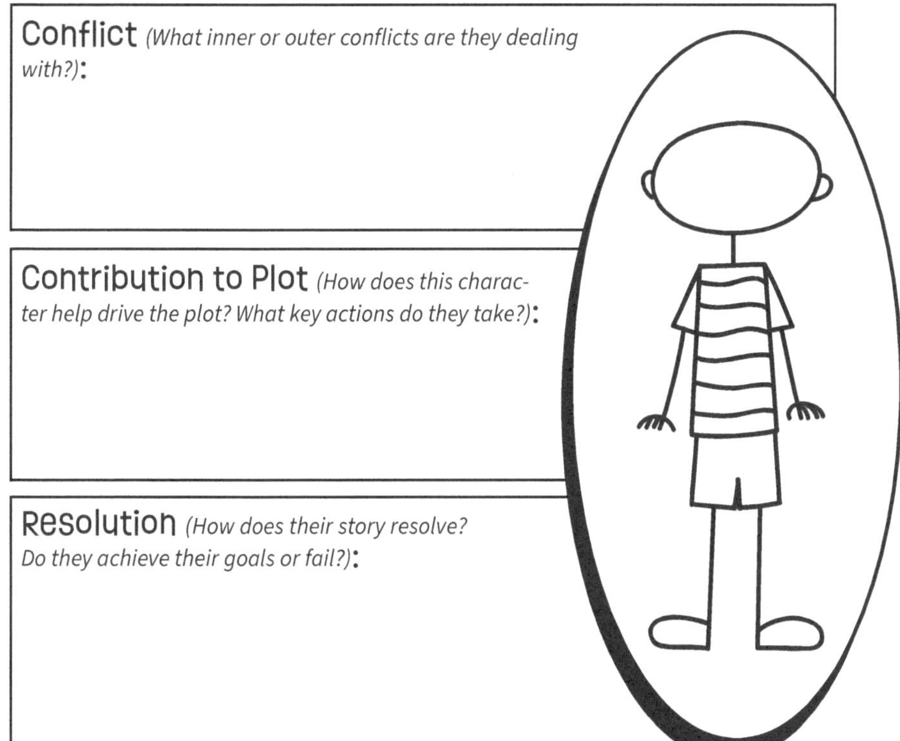

Conflict *(What inner or outer conflicts are they dealing with?)*:

Contribution to Plot *(How does this character help drive the plot? What key actions do they take?)*:

Resolution *(How does their story resolve? Do they achieve their goals or fail?)*:

STEP 4

Decide on Locations and Settings

Every mystery needs a place where the action happens. Think of your settings as the backdrop to your story's drama. Where do your characters live, work, and uncover clues? Make these places vivid in your mind—they'll help your mystery feel real.

STEP 4

Decide On Locations and Settings

Creating the Setting

THE SETTING OF YOUR STORY grounds it in a real time and place. When you create an interesting and specific setting, you give your characters a place to "set" the action and events of the story. Just like you "set" the table so that the spaghetti and meatballs aren't plopped onto a big blank table cloth, a writer "sets" the story background and creates the places to hold the story.

If we take the whole "setting the table" analogy further, you don't put out a plate and fork when your mom makes tomato soup, right? That wouldn't work and soup would run everywhere! In stories, the setting needs to fit with your story and be the right place for your story and characters to act out their tale.

In a mystery, the setting is often closely-linked to the kind of mystery, or sub-genre, it is. Cozy mysteries usually take place in small towns or villages, where everyone knows everyone else and the cast of characters is fairly small. Obviously, locked room mysteries happen in a place where everyone is trapped together for some reason. It may be a weekend party at a country manor house, or it could be a group of people stuck together on a yacht. Police procedurals often take place in a big city with lots of crime. You get the picture. Your particular type of mystery will help to determine what kind of setting you will have.

Remember, setting isn't just *where* the story happens but also *when* it happens. You can set your story today, in the current time (this is called a "contemporary" story), or you can set your story in a certain time period from the past, such as the late 1800s (this is called a "historical" story). You can also set your story in the future, but this isn't usually done with mysteries, unless it is both a mystery and a science fiction or fantasy story. You don't have to tell us, "It was London in the 1800s." Maybe you can show a carriage instead, and some fog hanging around the base of Big Ben. Use details of the setting as clues to let your reader know where and when the story takes place.

Whether you are writing a mystery or another kind of story, the goal of a good setting should be to create a world that is vivid and real, one that your readers can enter into and experience from within. Setting isn't just about the bigger world of your story, such as a village or a yacht, it is also about the physical places where each scene takes place.

You may be ready to head off and start writing, but wait a minute! Here are two setting pitfalls to especially watch out for:

A Setting that is Too Generic

Let's say you want to set your story on a beach. Don't just say, "Addie went to the beach," and then start your scene. Your job is to help your readers feel like they are at a particular beach. Think about the five senses: taste, touch, sound, sight, and smell. Show your readers what *this* particular beach is like. Is it rocky or sandy? What does it feel like under Addie's feet? What kind of smells are there? Dead fish? Salt water? What does Addie see when she looks around? Trees and logs and driftwood, or tall grasses growing around the edge of the sand? Does she hear seagulls? Barking dogs playing? Is the beach crowded or deserted?

Do you see how many questions come up when I just say beach? Sure, the word beach brings to mind some kind of image for most of us. But if I am reading your story and start to paint a certain beach, say a rocky one, and then you tell me a little later on that the beach is smooth, we have a problem. Now I have to mentally erase my first beach and create a whole new one. As readers, we are pretty good at adapting as we go along, but still, that moment pulls me out of the story. And guess what? If you pull your readers out of the story too many times, they are bound to get crabby, whether they're on a beach with crabs or not.

A Setting that is TOO Detailed

It is easy to over-write description for your setting. You don't want to be vague, so you think, "Okay, I will just spend a whole three paragraphs showing what the beach is like. I will use all the senses. Problem solved!" There's only one problem. Have you ever read three paragraphs describing a beach? It's BORING!

How do you create a setting that is vivid and detailed, but not bore your readers to tears with too much description? I'm glad you asked! It actually is quite simple. You show vivid details, but you only choose a few. You choose the best details that show your setting, maybe two or three. I don't need to paint a picture of every rock and part of the beach when describing my setting. Most readers know what a rocky beach looks like. So, give your readers a couple specific details that ground your scene, and trust they can handle the rest.

Another thing to consider is finding the right details for your point of view character. It may seem weird that setting has anything to do with your characters, but think about it. Different people notice different things. What things would a detective notice when entering a new place? I bet it's different than what you or I would notice. They might see the beach and notice how a section of the beach is missing rocks. Was it scraped clean to hide something? They might meet someone and pick up on the fact the person is smiling, all the while picking at the hole in their jeans. Are they nervous?

Remember also, the details you choose to show about your setting add to the tone and feel of your story. No one will think you are writing a cheery tale if you set it on a foggy dock at midnight. Similarly, it's hard to imagine a hard-boiled noir detective following up on a lead at a beauty parlour mid-morning on a sunny day. Time of day and the weather are very important to consider. Obviously, thunder and lightning feel a little scary, but what about a heat wave, where everyone is miserable and short on patience? Think about how your characters might act differently under the various stressful circumstances your setting can create.

One last thing. As you create the setting for your mystery, can you make the setting an important part of the mystery itself? What about making your interesting details also clues! Brainstorm how you can hide clues within the setting of your story. Perhaps the fact that the door handle sticks at the manor house will prove to be important. Maybe the location of different characters' rooms at the party will be the key to your detective figuring out "whodunnit." There are, literally, a world of possibilities when it comes to hiding clues in your setting.

STEP 5

Choose the Point-of-View

Who's telling your story? Choosing the right point of view is like picking the lens through which your readers will see the world you've created. Decide who's holding the camera, and watch your story come into focus!

STEP 5

Choose the Point-of-View

POV

HAVE YOU EVER listened to two people tell the same story? Did they tell it the same way, or did they emphasise different things? I bet if your grandma told the story of the day she fell in the pool, she would tell it differently than if you told it. That is because different narrators notice different things, and we all filter our experiences through other factors: how we feel, past experiences we've had, pre-conceived ideas, etc. Your grandma might include the fact she was distracted by the little dog barking around her feet, just before she fell in the water. You might tell how funny she looked as she fell.

Point-of-view in writing refers to who is telling the story, and from where. I'll explain.

There are three main points-of-view, or POV, used in fiction. This goes for mysteries too.

First Person

First person point-of-view is where a character, usually the main character, is telling the story. This POV uses pronouns like "I," "me," and "my," which helps readers deeply connect with the narrator's experiences and emotions. One of the strengths of first person POV is its ability to convey the narrator's voice and personality directly to the reader. This can make the reader feel close to the character, creating a very intimate and immersive experience.

However, the story is confined to the narrator's perspective, so the readers are restricted to that character's knowledge and experiences. This means that events happening outside the narrator's awareness remain unknown to the readers until the narrator learns about them. This limitation can be used to build suspense and surprise, but it requires careful planning to reveal key information at the right moments.

Some Books Written in First Person

Percy Jackson & The Olympians by Rick Riordan
The Hunger Games by Suzanne Collins
Diary of a Wimpy Kid by Jeff Kinney
Twilight by Stephenie Meyer

Third Person Limited

In third person limited POV, an outside narrator, not a character, tells the story but is limited to what one character can see, know, and experience. For example, the narrator follows one particular character, almost always the main character. If it's "close" third person POV, the narrator can also know what the character is thinking and feeling, but just this one character. The narrator can't tell us what the villain is doing across town if the POV character is not there.

One of the strengths of third person limited POV is its ability to convey the chosen character's thoughts and emotions to the reader, making them feel close to the character. However, the story is confined to this character's perspective, so the readers are restricted to that character's knowledge and experiences. This means that events happening outside the character's awareness remain unknown to the readers until the character learns about them. This balance of intimacy and limitation keeps the focus on the main character while maintaining narrative flexibility.

Some Books Written in Third Person Limited

The Harry Potter books by J.K. Rowling
The Maze Runner by James Dashner
The Giver by Lois Lowry
Coraline by Neil Gaiman

Third Person Omniscient

In third person omniscient POV, an outside narrator, not a character, tells the story, but this narrator knows everything about all the characters and events. This means the narrator can reveal what any character is thinking, feeling, and doing at any time. For example, the narrator can tell us what the detective is thinking and feeling, then jump across town and tell us something about the villain and what they are thinking.

To keep things straight, the narrator usually sticks with one POV character per scene or chapter. If you jump around from line to line into different characters' heads, that's called "head-hopping," and it gets pretty confusing to your readers! One of the strengths of third person omniscient POV is its ability to provide a comprehensive view of the story, offering insights into multiple characters and events. This allows readers to understand the broader context and see how different pieces of the puzzle fit together.

Some Books Written in Third Person Omniscient

Charlotte's Web by E.B. White
The Lion, the Witch and the Wardrobe by C.S. Lewis
The Adventures of Tom Sawyer by Mark Twain
Anne of Green Gables by L.M. Montgomery

As you plan your story, you need to decide which POV you will use. Remember also, who will tell the story and what POV you use will change the tone, or feel, of the story, and the experience your readers have.

Here are your options, with examples:

If you want your readers to feel close to your detective and right there with them as the mystery unfolds... you might choose first person POV. In first person, the detective will directly tell the story, such as "I walked into the room and saw the body. It made me remember my first case."

If you want your readers to feel close to your detective, but want an outside narrator... you might try third person limited. With this POV, your narrator will tell the story, but still stay close to your detective. It would read like, "Detective Jones walked into the room and saw the body. It made her remember her first case."

If you want your readers to feel close to your detective, but you still want to show scenes where your detective or POV character isn't there... you might try third person omniscient. In this POV you could say, "Detective Jones walked into the room and saw the body. It made her remember her first case.

Meanwhile, across town, Randolph Wilson ran down an alley out of breath. How had he not seen the danger before now? His mind raced wildly. He had to warn the professor before it was too late."

How to Choose Which POV to use?

You may feel stuck trying to decide between first person POV and third person POV (whether limited, omniscient). Don't worry! Here are some tips:

What do you enjoy reading?

Do you naturally gravitate to a book written in first person or third? Is there a kind of POV you don't like very much? Take a moment to think about it.

What do you find yourself naturally writing?

Do you instantly start writing as if you are the character living out the action of the story? If so, you naturally gravitate toward first person.

Or, perhaps you like to write about and notice things your characters might not notice yet. Maybe you find it easier to write in third person and that feels more natural. Whatever feels the best to you, start there. Chances are, you already lean toward one POV over another. There is no point trying to force yourself to write one way just because you think you should. Certainly, try out all the POVs and have fun! But in the end, pick what feels the easiest and most natural to you.

Does your story seem like it should be told directly or through a narrator?

Each story can be different. Just because you usually write in first person doesn't mean your next story has to use the same POV. As with most choices in writing, what best serves the story is the question you should ask.

Does your genre use one POV over another?

Many cozy mysteries use first person POV, but third person POV is also a popular choice for mysteries, as the narrator can show information that the characters may not be aware of yet.

Choosing WHO Will Tell Your Story

If you decide to use first person POV (or third person limited), you must decide which character will be narrating the story (or which character the POV "camera" is limited to). Many mystery stories in first person use the main character, the detective, to tell the story, but don't forget, you can also use a side character, or peripheral narrator, to tell the story. This is the case with the Sherlock Holmes stories, which are all told by Watson in first person POV. This can be a great technique, especially if you want your detective to seem a bit mysterious or hard to understand.

Another option is to tell your mystery from the first person POV of the villain. That can make an interesting story for sure! In this case, you would not reveal everything the villain thinks or does. In order to preserve the mystery, your readers could find out clues and information only when your detective uncovers them. Your readers might enjoy a peek into your villain's inner world. They would experience the villain's triumphant thoughts, as well the frustration and fear the villain feels as the detective closes in on them.

Take some time to decide on the POV that works best for you as a writer and for your story. Maybe even try a few out and see which one you like best.

Examples

To understand how different narrative perspectives can affect the reader's experience, consider the following example set in a bustling town square where Mr Thompson is searching for his missing hat. Each paragraph below is written from a different point of view, showcasing how the same scene can be shown through the eyes of different characters:

Third Person Omniscient

In the heart of the bustling town square, everyone could see Mr Thompson's frustration as he searched for his missing hat. Little did he know, young Lucy, hidden behind a nearby bench, had seen the hat tumble from his head and land beneath the fountain. While Mr Thompson's irritation grew with every passing moment, Lucy, feeling a pang of guilt, debated whether to reveal what she had witnessed. Meanwhile, Mrs Parker, sipping her tea from the café across the street, was oblivious to the unfolding drama and instead focused on her latest novel.

Third Person Limited

Mr Thompson's frustration was evident as he scoured the town square for his missing hat. His mind raced with thoughts of how he would explain the loss to his wife. He saw his young neighbour, Lucy, crouched behind a bench and wondered if she might know what happened to it. She was watching him intently. At the same time, he saw Mrs Parker sitting comfortably in the café, engrossed in her novel and unaware of his small crisis.

First Person (Mr Thompson)

I couldn't believe it—I'd lost my hat. I walked back and forth across the town square, my frustration mounting with each passing moment. I checked every possible place I could have left it, but it was nowhere to be found. I felt a wave of anxiety about how I'd explain this to my wife—how could I tell her I lost the birthday gift she'd given me last year? I saw Lucy watching me from behind a bench and wondered if her mother knew where she was. Meanwhile, over at the café, Mrs Parker looked like she had no idea of my dilemma; she was lost in her book, completely oblivious to my plight.

First Person (Lucy)

I peeked out from behind the bench, my heart racing as I watched Mr Thompson frantically searching for his hat. I had seen it fall into the fountain, but I wasn't sure if I should tell him. I felt guilty for not speaking up but I didn't want to draw attention to myself—Janet and Chris would never find me in this great hiding spot and I really wanted to finally win a game! From where I was, I could also see Mrs Parker across the street, oblivious to the whole situation as she read her book. I had to make a decision quickly before Mr Thompson left in frustration.

STEP 6

Plot the Story

Now that you've got the pieces, it's time to put the puzzle together! Plotting your story is like creating a skeleton for your mystery. Sketch out the twists and turns—this is where your detective work starts to pay off.

STEP 6

Plot the Story

Your Story's Skeleton

SOME OF YOU may be wondering what exactly "plot" is? It may sound a little confusing. Basically, the plot is everything that *happens* in your story, and just like life, things shouldn't happen all willy-nilly and out of order. There should be some structure. First you get up, brush your teeth, then get dressed. There is some freedom in how we structure things. Sure, you can get dressed first and *then* brush your teeth. But you can't brush your teeth before you get out of bed!

The events in your story should also unfold in a logical order. It's even better if you can make the events in your story build upon each other. That means when you get up from sleeping, you need to brush your teeth. I can have my character get up and play the accordion, but that would be a little random. Events that build on one another are related by cause and effect. In other words, something happens (I go to the movies), then another thing happens because of the first thing (I run into my old music teacher and learn her clarinet was stolen).

As you think about what happens in your story, try to ask yourself, "What happens next?" You are writing a mystery, so you already know how your book should start. There will be some kind of crime, a detective will be called or stumble onto the scene, your readers will get to know your detective as they assess the situation, and then other characters (suspects) will start to come into the story.

Plot is always based, ideally, on your characters striving to reach their goals. Your detective wants to solve the crime. Your villain? They want to get away with it! Since we know satisfying mysteries need to be complex and not obviously solved, we throw in other characters as suspects. We also lay out the clues carefully, and throw a few red herrings (false clues) in as well. We also might have side characters who create roadblocks for the detective. All of this just makes the detective and story more likable as we struggle to solve the crime.

So, how do you order your story? How do you begin?

It can help to look at story models, kind of like cake pans for creating a story. You can mix up batter and pour it out onto the counter, but it will go everywhere! If you pour your batter into a cake pan, you have everything contained into a nice shape. Then the cake can bake and become the cake it was meant to be.

Are you hungry for cake yet? Sorry, let's move past the cake! Your story is like this example. You combine all kinds of things into your "batter"—great characters, an interesting plot, a stellar setting—and then you take that story batter and pour it into a pan, in this case, a story structure.

What is a story structure? There are lots of them. The one we're going to focus on is a simple one called the Three-act Structure. You already know lots of stories with this format. At its most simple, the three-act structure is this: beginning, middle, end.

Within these three acts, we are going to have different key things happen in your story. This will help make sure the story flows well and we don't have characters brushing their teeth before they get out of bed. We call these key things "story beats." They are the different, important parts that a story with this structure needs to include.

The next few pages list all the elements you need for your structure and where to place them in your book.

Act 1

Opening

Here, we introduce the protagonist, or main character, and give the readers a feel for what kind of mystery it will be. This is where readers meet the main character and get a glimpse of their world, as well as the tone and style of the mystery. The key element here is the "hook"—an engaging or intriguing scene designed to grab the readers' attention immediately. Just like a fish on a hook, this captivating moment ensures they're drawn in and eager to keep turning the pages.

Setup

This section sets the stage for your story by introducing the world where your mystery unfolds. It should provide a glimpse into the setting, whether it's a school, neighbourhood, or another location. Here, you'll also meet other key characters, such as friends, family, or potential suspects, who will play important roles in the plot. Additionally, the setup hints at the central conflict or mystery, giving readers a taste of the problem that needs to be solved.

Inciting Incident

This is the moment that jump-starts the mystery and shakes up the detective's world. It's unexpected and packs a punch, setting the stage for everything that follows. Whether it's a shocking crime or a puzzling clue, this event disrupts the detective's normal life and pushes them to start investigating. It's the spark that gets them moving, making them determined to solve the mystery.

Call to Action

This is the pivotal instant when the detective must respond to the unfolding events. This step serves as the detective's invitation to engage with the mystery. It is the moment when the detective is called to act in some way and take part in solving the crime. For a professional detective, it might be the official assignment to the case. For an amateur sleuth, it could be the realisation that no one else is taking the crime seriously or noticing crucial details. This is when the detective decides to take action, stepping into their role and committing to solving the case.

Act 2

The Choice

The detective makes an active choice to throw themself fully into the case. For example, maybe they realise the death that everyone thinks is an accident is actually a murder, and they must act or the villain won't be stopped. This decision marks the point of no return, propelling the detective into the heart of the investigation.

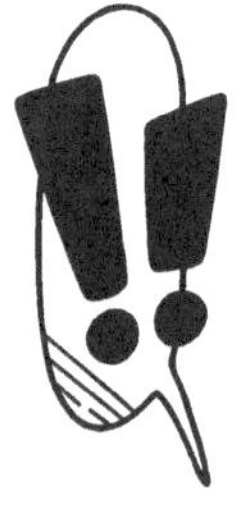

Try/Fail

The detective and friends/sidekicks try to solve the case. This section includes several scenes where they find clues, interview suspects and witnesses, and sometimes fall for red herrings. They fail a lot as things still don't add up, but also have some successes as they move toward solving the case.

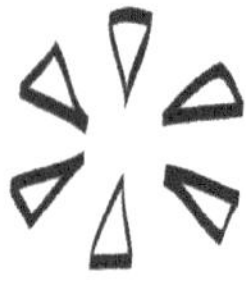

Midpoint

Some unexpected revelation sends the story in a new direction and the stakes are raised. This revelation sharpens their focus, new clues are uncovered and hidden motives are exposed. As the detective grapples with this new information, they move closer to unraveling the mystery, setting the stage for intensified conflict and bringing them nearer to confronting the villain.

Rising Threats

The detective keeps on the trail, but the villain now sees a serious threat and ramps up their attacks and roadblocks to the detective's efforts. Their sole focus now is to evade capture. They may, depending on the story, grow dangerous to either the detective or others as they become more and more threatened.

Dark Moment

The investigation hits a serious snag. The detective faces a frustrating setback: clues become confusing, the trail goes cold, or the villain seems to outmaneuver them. The detective might even discover that their prime suspect was a red herring all along. Overwhelmed and disheartened, the detective confronts the real possibility of failure, feeling as if the mystery is slipping through their fingers. This is the story's lowest point.

Turning Point

At this juncture, a breakthrough—a new clue, a fresh insight, or a critical puzzle piece—emerges, reigniting the detective's determination. They are back on the case!

Act 3

A New Plan

Energised by the fresh insights or newfound motivation from the Turning Point, the detective devises a revamped strategy to tackle the case and unmask the villain. With renewed determination, the detective refines their approach, setting up new tactics or revisiting old evidence with a fresh perspective. This stage marks a pivotal shift in the investigation.

Climax

This is the big moment of the whole story. It is what the action has been building toward. All the clues come together and the detective figures out who the villain really is and how to catch them. It's a thrilling moment, often leading to a big showdown or an intense face-off with the villain. This is the moment that the whole mystery has been building up to, and it's where everything finally clicks into place for the detective.

Resolution

After the Climax and the villain is safely in custody or no longer a threat, the detective wraps up the mystery by explaining everything. They reveal the villain's timeline (when and how they did each step of the plan), and also reveal the villain's motive for committing the crime.

A SIDE NOTE

Some authors find it easiest to work backwards. This is where you come up with the climax of your book first. In a mystery, this is the scene where your detective realises who the villain is (or how they did it and how to catch them). If you want to try this method, just fill in the worksheet starting out (or back) from the story beat that comes to you first.

The advantage to working from the end is that you have a clear idea of how your book will end and the place your story is building to. If this seems complicated, don't worry. You can also work out your story from beginning to end, and then change story beats to fit the ending you, well, end up with.

STEP 6

Plot the Story

Acts

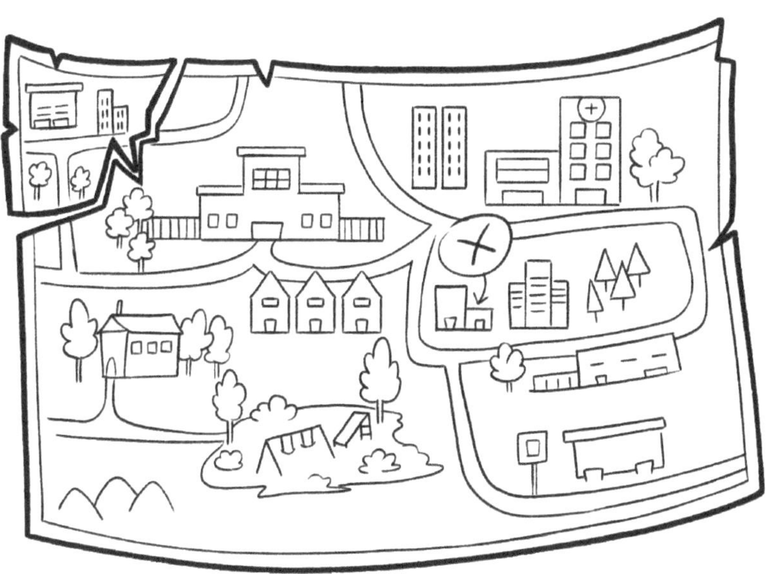

Getting Started!

TAKE A LOOK at the following worksheet. Get out your one-page story idea. Where do the events of your story naturally fit? Are you missing any beats? What can you add in to make sure there aren't any plot holes? Fill out the worksheet the best you can. Remember, this can also change and grow as you write your story. It is just helpful to have a plot structure as you write your book. For now, don't worry about planting clues and all of that. Just work out what should happen for each story beat.

ACT 1

THE BEGINNING

The Opening

Sets the tone for the story and introduces the detective.

Setup

Scenes that introduce the world and other important characters—friends, side-kicks, possible suspects.

Inciting Incident

The crime, clue, or event occurs that kicks off the story.

Call to Action

The moment when the detective is called to act in some way and take part in solving the crime. This can sometimes happen before the Setup.

ACT 2

THE MIDDLE – PART 1

The Choice

The detective makes an active choice to throw themself fully into the case.

Try/Fail

The detective and friends/side-kicks try to solve the case by finding clues, researching, interviewing suspects. Sometimes they fall for red herrings. They have some successes but mostly dead ends.

Midpoint

An unexpected revelation sends the story in a new direction and the stakes are raised. The detective gets closer to catching the villain.

ACT 2

THE MIDDLE – PART 2

Rising Threats

The detective keeps on the trail, but the villain now sees a serious threat and ramps up their attacks and roadblocks to the detective's efforts.

Dark Moment

The trail grows cold and the villain seems successful in outwitting the detective. The detective feels confused as clues don't add up.

Turning Point

Something offers hope (a new clue, insight, or puzzle piece) and the detective has renewed energy to keep going. They are back on the case!

ACT 3

THE END

A New Plan

Energised by the new info, the detective forms a new plan to catch the villain.

Climax

The detective puts the last piece together and suddenly knows who the villain is and how to catch them. There may also be a dramatic or dangerous encounter with the villain in a final confrontation.

Resolution

The villain no longer a threat and the detective reveals how the villain committed the crime and why.

At this point, you might be wondering how long to make your book, or maybe how much of your book should be in Act 1, 2, or 3? In the writing world, we use word counts instead of page counts. A typical word count for a middle grade novel is 25,000 to 65,000 words. The next section will show you how to divide your Acts into Chapters.

STEP 6

Plot the Story

Chapters

Just a Little Bit of Math

ARE YOU WORRIED about how you should divide all those words? Don't be! It's simple once you break it down. Let's work with an example for a novel on the shorter side: 30,000 words. To give you an idea how long that is, the novel *Charlie and the Chocolate Factory* has 30,644 words and *The Lion, the Witch, and the Wardrobe* has 36,363 words.

Let's make each chapter 1000 words. Ideally, your first act should be about 25% of your total book. Your second act is always the biggest so it should be 50% of the whole book. The third act is about the same length as your first act so it should also be 25%.

Act 1 = 7.5 chapters

Act 2 = 15 chapters

Act 3 = 7.5 chapters

Since we don't want to have half chapters, let's divide the acts up like this:

Act 1 = 7 chapters

Act 2 = 15 chapters (8 for the first half, 7 for the second half)

Act 3 = 8 chapters

The next pages give you a visual of how to break down your chapters.

Imagine the black bar is your novel

ACT 1
The Beginning

Introduce your characters and get the story started!

Divide **7** chapters between these story beats

- **Opening**
- **Setup**
- **Inciting Incident**
- **Call to Action**

Each chapter is about 1000 words

CHAPTER 1 | CHAPTER 2 | CHAPTER 3 | CHAPTER 4 | CHAPTER 5 | CHAPTER 6 | CHAPTER 7

Break up each chapter with 1 to 3 scenes

ACT 2
PART ONE
The Middle

The hero decides to go for it but soon realises things are harder than they seem.

Divide **8** chapters between these story beats

- **The Choice**
- **Try/Fail**
- **Midpoint**

Each chapter is about 1000 words

CHAPTER 8 | CHAPTER 9 | CHAPTER 10 | CHAPTER 11 | CHAPTER 12 | CHAPTER 13 | CHAPTER 14 | CHAPTER 15

Break up each chapter with 1 to 3 scenes

Scenes are mini-stories that link together to make your book. Like the book itself, each scene needs a beginning, middle, and end.

Act 2 is the biggest part of your book and is divided into two parts. Together, all of Act 2 makes up 50% of your book, or 15 chapters. Divide the 15 chapters any way you think is best.

ACT 2

PART TWO

The Middle

The villain almost crushes the hero, who starts to lose hope. But wait...

Divide **7** chapters between these story beats

- **Rising Threats**
- **Dark Moment**
- **Turning Point**

Each chapter is about 1000 words

CHAPTER 16 | CHAPTER 17 | CHAPTER 18 | CHAPTER 19 | CHAPTER 20 | CHAPTER 21 | CHAPTER 22

Break up each chapter with 1 to 3 scenes

ACT 3

End

The hero comes up with a plan that turns things around. And...VICTORY!

Divide **8** chapters between these story beats

- **A New Plan**
- **Climax**
- **Resolution**

Each chapter is about 1000 words

CHAPTER 23 | CHAPTER 24 | CHAPTER 25 | CHAPTER 26 | CHAPTER 27 | CHAPTER 28 | CHAPTER 29 | CHAPTER 30

Break up each chapter with 1 to 3 scenes

This way of breaking down your novel is just a guide. You can have as many (or as few!) chapters and words as you want.

Each chapter = 1000 words

Each chapter = 1 to 3 scenes

With your story beats laid out, it's time to dive deeper into the details by breaking down each act into chapters and specific story beats. This exercise will help you organise the flow of your story, making sure that each chapter serves a clear purpose and moves the plot forward.

By mapping out the key events in each chapter, you'll create an even more detailed framework for your story that guides your writing and keeps the pacing tight. The next few pages show you an example of how to do just that.

TIP

Think of each chapter as its own mini-mystery. It should have a beginning, middle, and end, with just enough intrigue to keep your readers hungry for the next one. Keep the suspense rolling, and your readers will be hooked until the very last page!

Act One
(7 Chapters)

Opening

CHAPTER 1: Meet Our Hero—Introduce the main character, a detective.

Setup

CHAPTER 2: A Quiet Day—Show the detective's daily life and introduce their friends.
CHAPTER 3: The Detective's Hobby—Reveal the detective's love for solving puzzles and mysteries.

Inciting Incident

CHAPTER 4: The Big Surprise—Something valuable goes missing, and everyone is worried.
CHAPTER 5: Gathering Clues—The detective starts looking for clues around the scene.

Call to Action

CHAPTER 6: Meet the Suspects—Introduce a few characters who might have taken the missing item.
CHAPTER 7: The Challenge—The detective decides to take on the case and solve the mystery.

Act Two (Part 1)
(8 Chapters)

The Choice

CHAPTER 8: A Tough Decision—The detective decides to investigate each suspect thoroughly.

Try/Fail

CHAPTER 9: The First Interview—The detective questions the first suspect but finds nothing.
CHAPTER 10: More Questions—The detective interviews more suspects but still has no answers.
CHAPTER 11: A Wrong Turn—The detective follows a false lead and feels frustrated.
CHAPTER 12: Another Clue—The detective finds a small clue that keeps the hope alive.

Midpoint

CHAPTER 13: A Big Break—The detective discovers something important that changes everything.
CHAPTER 14: New Leads—The detective follows new leads but still can't solve the mystery.
CHAPTER 15: Pressure Builds—The detective feels the pressure as time runs out.

Act Two (Part 2)
(7 Chapters)

Rising Threats

CHAPTER 16: Suspect in Danger—One of the suspects seems to be in trouble, raising the stakes.

CHAPTER 17: The Secret—The detective uncovers a secret that one of the suspects was hiding.

CHAPTER 18: Unexpected Help—A friend offers a surprising piece of information.

Dark Moment

CHAPTER 19: Feeling Defeated—The detective hits a dead end and feels like giving up.

CHAPTER 20: A Sad Day—The detective struggles with the thought of not solving the mystery.

Turning Point

CHAPTER 21: A Fresh Idea—The detective gets a new idea from an unexpected place.

CHAPTER 22: The Final Clue—The detective finds one last clue that points to the real culprit.

Act Three
(8 Chapters)

A New Plan

CHAPTER 23: Connecting the Dots—The detective starts to piece everything together.

CHAPTER 24: The Big Plan—The detective makes a plan to catch the culprit.

Climax

CHAPTER 25: The Trap—The detective sets the trap and waits.

CHAPTER 26: Narrow Escape—The detective avoids a tricky situation before the final confrontation.

CHAPTER 27: The Confrontation—The culprit falls into the trap and is confronted.

Resolution

CHAPTER 28: The Truth Revealed—The detective reveals how they solved the mystery.

CHAPTER 29: Celebrations—Everyone celebrates the detective's success.

CHAPTER 30: A New Beginning—The detective looks forward to new mysteries.

While the story structure I've provided is a great starting point for building your mystery, remember that storytelling is a creative process. It's perfectly okay to deviate from this formula as you develop your story. The story beats don't always have to follow the exact order listed. Sometimes, a particular story might benefit from mixing things up a bit to keep readers engaged and intrigued. The key is to ensure that your story flows naturally and keeps your audience hooked from start to finish.

The next example takes the same story but mixes up a few of the story beats and goes into even more detail.

TIP

Story structure isn't about rigid rules you have to follow, but it can be helpful to new writers (and old ones) to make sure the story doesn't miss out on the key elements that most satisfying stories have.

Act One

CHAPTER 1 | The Crime | Inciting Incident

Boom! Something shocking happens that kicks off the mystery. Maybe it's a robbery, a disappearance, or a strange event. Whatever it is, it leaves behind some tantalising clues.

CHAPTER 2 | Meet the Detective | Opening

Introduce our hero! This could be a clever kid with a knack for solving puzzles, or a young sleuth with a unique talent. Give readers a glimpse of their background and what makes them awesome.

CHAPTER 3 | The Investigation Begins | Setup

Our detective dives into the case, starting with the crime scene. They begin to gather the initial clues, piecing together the first parts of the mystery.

CHAPTER 4 | Meet Potential Suspects | Setup

Time to meet the suspects! Each one should have a possible motive and something interesting about them that makes readers wonder if they did it.

CHAPTER 5 | New Information | Call to Action
The plot thickens! Reveal more details about the crime that make it even more puzzling and intriguing, pushing the detective to dig deeper.

CHAPTER 6 | Detective's Private Life | Setup
Peek into the detective's personal world. Maybe they have a quirky hobby, a tricky relationship, or a secret of their own. This subplot adds depth and makes the detective more relatable.

CHAPTER 7 | A Break in the Case | The Choice
Bingo! The detective stumbles upon a promising lead or clue that propels the investigation forward. This is the moment that sets up the thrilling transition to Act Two.

TIP

When introducing your detective, make sure to showcase their unique qualities and skills. What makes them special? Whether it's a keen eye for detail, an unusual hobby that helps solve crimes, or a quirky personality, these traits will help readers connect with your detective and root for them throughout the story.

Act Two (Part 1)

CHAPTER 8 | Investigating Suspects | Try/Fail

The detective starts questioning the suspects, digging into their backgrounds, and uncovering their secrets. Some suspects might have airtight alibis, while others seem suspicious.

CHAPTER 9 | Gathering Clues | Try/Fail

Clues start piling up! The detective finds more pieces of the puzzle, though not all of them make sense right away.

CHAPTER 10 | Witness Testimonies | Try/Fail

Time to talk to witnesses. They provide conflicting accounts, adding to the mystery and making it even harder to figure out who's telling the truth.

CHAPTER 11 | Suspect Disappears | Rising Threats

Uh-oh! One of the suspects vanishes, creating a sense of urgency and raising the stakes. Is this person hiding something, or are they in danger?

CHAPTER 12 | Subplot Development | Setup

Develop the detective's personal subplot further. Perhaps their private life gets tangled up in the case, adding an emotional layer to the story.

CHAPTER 13 | Stakes Are Raised | Rising Threats

The detective learns something that makes solving the crime even more critical. Maybe there's a new deadline, or someone else is at risk. The pressure is on!

CHAPTER 14 | Detective's Dilemma | Try/Fail

The detective faces a tough choice or a moral quandary related to the case. This moment challenges their resolve and tests their character.

TIP

In the first half of Act 2, focus on building suspense. Use cliffhangers at the end of chapters to keep readers eager to turn the page. As your detective gathers clues and questions suspects, throw in red herrings and false leads to keep the mystery intriguing and unpredictable.

Act Two (Part 2)

CHAPTER 15 | Close Call | Rising Threats

Things get intense! The detective narrowly escapes danger, whether it's a trap set by the villain or a risky situation that almost goes wrong.

CHAPTER 16 | Unexpected Ally | Turning Point

Help comes from an unexpected place. An unlikely character offers crucial assistance, giving the detective new hope and a fresh perspective.

CHAPTER 17 | New Suspect Emerges | Try/Fail

Just when things seem clear, a new suspect comes into the picture, turning the investigation on its head and adding to the suspense.

CHAPTER 18 | A Dead End | Dark Moment

The detective hits a frustrating dead end. The trail goes cold, and it seems like the mystery might never be solved.

CHAPTER 19 | Personal Stakes | Rising Threats

The case takes a toll on the detective's personal life, making the stakes even higher. They might face consequences or challenges that affect them deeply.

CHAPTER 20 | A Hidden Connection | Midpoint

A hidden link between suspects or clues is revealed, changing everything. This discovery sharpens the detective's focus and brings new clarity.

CHAPTER 21 | Tension Escalates | Rising Threats

The villain amps up their efforts to throw the detective off the trail. New obstacles and threats make the investigation even more dangerous.

CHAPTER 22 | Subplot Climax | Midpoint

The detective's personal subplot reaches a climax, intertwining with the main mystery and adding another layer of excitement.

TIP

In the second half of Act 2, raise the stakes and increase the tension. Show how the mystery affects the detective personally, and how the villain's actions become more dangerous. This will keep readers on the edge of their seats and make the final resolution even more satisfying.

Act Three

CHAPTER 23 | Secrets Unveiled | Rising Threats

Major secrets about the suspects and the crime are uncovered, dramatically altering the course of the investigation and bringing the detective closer to the truth.

CHAPTER 24 | False Resolution | Dark Moment

It seems like the detective has solved the case, but something still doesn't add up. This false resolution leads to a deeper understanding of the mystery.

CHAPTER 25 | Trail Goes Cold | Dark Moment

The investigation stalls again, and the detective feels a sense of defeat. This is their lowest point, where giving up seems almost inevitable.

CHAPTER 26 | Overlooked Clue | Turning Point

The detective revisits an overlooked clue from Act One, and suddenly, it all makes sense. This breakthrough reignites their determination.

CHAPTER 27 | Last Piece of the Puzzle | A New Plan

The last crucial clue is found, revealing the villain's identity and motive. The detective forms a solid plan to catch the culprit.

CHAPTER 28 | Showdown with the Villain | Climax

The thrilling climax! The detective confronts the villain in a dramatic showdown where all is revealed. The tension peaks as the mystery is solved.

CHAPTER 29 | Resolution | Resolution

The villain is caught, and the case is closed. The detective reflects on the adventure, hinting at future mysteries to come.

CHAPTER 30 | Subplot Resolution | Resolution

The detective's personal subplot is tied up, providing closure and showing how the case has affected their life. It›s a satisfying end that leaves readers eager for more.

TIP

As you move into Act 3, focus on delivering a satisfying conclusion. Make sure all the clues come together logically, and the detective's final revelation feels earned. The showdown with the villain should be thrilling, but also ensure the resolution ties up loose ends and leaves readers with a sense of closure.

Now that you've seen a couple of examples of how to structure a mystery story, it's your turn to create a chapter outline! Use the template on the next few pages to map out your story, or use a notebook if you need more room. Look at your one-page story and your plot worksheet to guide you.

Make a list of chapters under each Act and one or two sentences about what will happen in that chapter. It doesn't have to be perfect! This list will probably change as you write your book, but it will give you something to work with.

Keep in mind the acts and essential story beats, but don't be afraid to switch things up if your story needs it. Remember, while it's helpful to follow the structure provided, don't be afraid to add your own creative twists and turns. For example, you might reveal the villain's identity earlier in the story, turning the rest of the mystery into a tense game of cat and mouse. Or, you might decide to start your story with a dramatic reveal of the crime, and then use flashbacks to show how it all happened. Creating this outline will bring your mystery to life, chapter by chapter.

CHAPTER OUTLINE

ACT 1 THE BEGINNING

Divide 7 chapters between the four sections

The Opening	Setup	Inciting Incident	Call to Action
Sets the tone for the story and introduces the detective.	Scenes that introduce the world and other important characters: friends, side-kicks, possible suspects.	The crime, clue, or event occurs that kicks off the story.	The moment when the detective is called to act in some way and take part in solving the crime.

CHAPTER OUTLINE

ACT 2 THE MIDDLE - PART 1

Divide 7 chapters between the three sections

The Choice

The detective makes an active choice to throw themself fully into the case.

Try/Fail

The detective finds some clues but may fall for a red herring (or more). They have some successes but mostly dead ends.

Midpoint

An unexpected revelation sends the story in a new direction and the stakes are raised. The detective grows closer to catching the villain.

CHAPTER OUTLINE

ACT 2

THE MIDDLE - PART 2

Divide 8 chapters between the three sections

Rising Threats

The detective keeps on the trail, but the villain roadblocks the detective's efforts.

Dark Moment

The trail grows cold and the villain seems successful in outwitting the detective. The detective feels confused as clues don't add up.

Turning Point

Something offers hope (a new clue, insight, or puzzle piece) and the detective has renewed energy to keep going. They are back on the case!

CHAPTER OUTLINE

ACT 3 THE END

Divide 8 chapters between the three sections

A New Plan

Energised by the new info, the detective forms a new plan to catch the villain.

Climax

The detective puts the last piece together. There may be a dramatic encounter with the villain in a final confrontation.

Resolution

The villain no longer a threat and the detective reveals how the villain committed the crime and why.

Creating Scenes Within Your Chapters

NOW THAT YOU'VE DEVELOPED your chapter outline, it's time to dive deeper into your story. Each chapter is made up of scenes that bring your plot to life. Not sure what a scene is? A scene is anytime you are moving locations in your story or finishing up one small section and moving on to another one. They're the building blocks of your chapters, each one moving the story forward and developing your characters.

Creating a scene is like building a mini-story within your larger narrative. Each scene has a purpose, drives the plot forward, and develops your characters.

When breaking up your chapters into scenes, think of each scene as a piece of a puzzle. Every piece needs to fit perfectly to reveal the complete picture of your story. Start by asking yourself: What do I want to achieve in this chapter? Then, break it down into smaller goals, each represented by a scene.

Scenes can vary in length, but they should all serve a purpose. Whether it's revealing an important clue, introducing a new character, or showing the hero's reaction to a twist, each scene should contribute to the overall plot or character development. If a scene doesn't move the story forward or reveal something new, it might be time to rethink its place in your chapter.

Also, pay attention to the pacing. Scenes with lots of action might be shorter and faster, keeping readers on the edge of their seats. On the other hand, scenes where characters reflect or make important decisions might be longer, giving readers time to absorb the information.

Transitions between scenes are important, too. They should flow smoothly, guiding the reader from one moment to the next without jarring shifts. Think about how the end of one scene can set up the next, creating a natural progression that keeps the reader hooked.

Finally, think about how your characters are feeling and changing in each scene. This is your chance to show their emotions and reactions to what's happening around them. By highlighting these emotional moments, you'll make your story more engaging and relatable for your readers.

Purpose of the Scene

Ask Yourself:

Why is this scene important?

Function

Does it advance the plot, reveal character traits, create tension, or provide important information?

Goal

Every scene should have a clear goal, whether it's finding a clue, having a critical conversation, or encountering an obstacle.

Setting the Scene

Location

Where is the scene taking place? Is it a familiar place to the characters or somewhere new and intriguing?

Atmosphere

Use descriptive language to set the mood. Is it a dark, stormy night or a bright, bustling market?

Details

"Sensory details" (sights, sounds, smells) are crucial in helping to immerse the reader in the setting, making the scene more vivid and engaging.

Character Actions and Dialogue

Actions

What are the characters doing? Their actions should reflect their goals and personalities.

Dialogue

Conversations should be purposeful, revealing information or advancing the plot. Keep them natural and authentic to each character's voice.

Body Language

Non-verbal cues can add depth to interactions and show emotions.

Conflict and Tension

Internal Conflict

What is the character thinking or feeling? Are they conflicted or anxious?

External Conflict

What challenges or obstacles do they face in this scene? Conflict drives the narrative and keeps readers engaged.

Remember, each beat doesn't have to equal one chapter. Yes, your Opening might be one chapter, but your Setup section might be several chapters.

Pacing and Structure

Beginning

Start the scene with something engaging—a piece of action, intriguing dialogue, or a vivid description.

Middle

Develop the scene by building tension, revealing information, or showing character interactions.

End

Conclude the scene with a cliffhanger, a new revelation, or a turning point that leads to the next scene.

Linking Scenes Together

Transitions

Smoothly connect scenes to maintain the flow of the story. Use a character's thoughts, a piece of dialogue, or a new piece of action to transition.

Consistency

Ensure that each scene logically follows the previous one and sets up the next.

A good rule of thumb is to have at least 1-3 scenes in a chapter. This keeps the story moving and gives readers enough action and detail without overwhelming them. Each scene should advance the plot, develop characters, or reveal important information.

When to End a Chapter

Now that you've got a handle on creating scenes that drive your story forward and bring your characters to life, it's time to think about how to wrap up each chapter. Just like a good scene has a purpose, the way you end a chapter is crucial for keeping your readers hooked and eager to find out what happens in the next.

Most writers, because we start as readers, already have a built-in sense for where chapters should end. You know your story! Where are the natural pauses? Trust your instincts when it comes to chapter breaks.

If you still need help, here are a few tips for deciding where to put in chapter endings.

When you finish a scene or scenes

Not all scenes need to be a whole chapter. In fact, most chapters are made up of multiple scenes. You might have a small scene where your detective needs to run into the store and find out what a suspect purchased on the day of the crime. But what if this scene is only a few hundred words? Should it be an entire chapter? No, it can just be a scene. After the scene, you can jump down two lines and start a new scene, still in the same chapter. But, if your scene is already pretty long, or you feel you are going off on a new story beat or part of the novel, that might be a good place to end your chapter.

When you've reached your chapter word count

Use your word count as a helpful guide as you write. It isn't a rule, but it can help you keep your chapters roughly the same length. If you are trying to make each chapter around 1,000 words (and you are at 950 words and about to start a whole new scene), end your chapter and start the next section in a new one. If you only have 250 words and need to go to a new scene, you can just drop down two lines (hit enter twice) and start your new scene without ending the chapter.

When you've just finished some exciting moment

Ending a chapter on a cliffhanger, or when your readers can't wait to see what happens next, is one way to make sure your readers come back to your story. It's a great way to speed up the pace and intensity of your book and keep things exciting. Cliffhangers are where you leave something "hanging" at the end of the chapter—sometimes it's your main character literally hanging off a cliff, but usually it's some key piece of information that's hinted at but not revealed. By setting up these mini-mysteries, you keep your readers eager to flip on to the next chapter.

Don't perfectly resolve everything in each chapter. End it right as something is revealed, or about to be. Finding out new information about the case, or having a lead you thought was going somewhere suddenly fall flat, are good "cliffhanger" material. Sometimes you can even drop a bomb of new information right at the end of the chapter, but not show everyone's reactions to it. Your readers will be dying to know what your characters think and do with the new information and will read on to the next chapter.

Now you know how to break up your novel into all its story and structural parts. Think of your book like a skyscraper—an impressive structure that stands tall because of the careful assembly of its beams, glass, and countless screws. Each part plays a crucial role in holding the building together and giving it its shape. Similarly, your story is built from Acts, Chapters, and Scenes. The Acts provide the framework, the Chapters create the floors, and the Scenes are like the rooms filled with the details that bring your story to life. When you put all these parts together thoughtfully, they form a strong, captivating story that your readers can't put down.

TIP

Remember, every part of your story—characters, plot, clues, and settings—works together like pieces of a puzzle to create a great mystery. Just like a detective pieces together clues, make sure each element in your story connects seamlessly to build suspense and keep readers guessing until the very end!

STEP 7

Plan the Villain's Timeline

Your villain is up to something, and it's your job to map it out. Track every sneaky move they make. By planning their timeline, you'll keep your mystery tight and thrilling. Get ready to stay one step ahead!

STEP 7

Plan the Villain's Timeline

The Villain's Sneaky Moves

THE CRIME OF YOUR MYSTERY novel is *the* main event of your whole story. Think about it! Everything that happens before, during, and after your story revolves around the crime. You need to know the crime inside and out.

Let's take a moment to brainstorm this central part of your whole story. What is it (a murder, a theft, a kidnapping)? Who does it happen to (who is the victim)? Who is the villain committing the crime? Why do they commit this crime (revenge, hatred, self-defense, greed, fear, etc.)? Where does the crime occur? When does it happen? Does the crime happen as "backstory" (as in, before the start of your story), or does it happen after your story has already started?

As you know, mystery stories are all about the details, both real clues and false ones that lead the readers off on a wild goose chase. But to write a story brimming with details, you need to know everything about the crime that was committed.

Creating a timeline of the events of the crime, and where the actions of the villain fall, will ensure that everything adds up and falls where it should. This information is just for you, only to be revealed right at the end when the hero solves the mystery. Think of it as the master key to your whole story.

A mystery novel is like a finely woven tapestry. On the surface, it appears as a beautiful picture—think of this as your plot and characters. But behind the scenes, countless threads of different colours and textures come together to create the intricate design. You are the "weaver" of your story, carefully threading the details of your villain's actions and motives. This careful craftsmanship may not be visible to your readers, but the rich, layered storytelling will create a captivating mystery that draws in your readers.

You may be wondering why you need to worry about things that happen that never show up in your story? Let's take a look at an example story to show you why things that happen before your story starts can be very important.

First, read the story. Then, I will reveal some backstory information (that would come out later on if this was a novel).

Here's the story:

Jenn just had to find out who stole Derek's new bike. He had worked so hard to save for it! As she walked into the park, she glanced at her watch—3:35. Marty should be somewhere. She spotted him by the picnic tables. Surely Marty didn't do it, but she had to rule out all the possibilities.

Jenn ran over. "Hey! Thanks for meeting me."

Marty nodded stiffly. He sat with his back to the kids splashing in the pool.

Jenn plopped down. "So, some day at the fair yesterday, huh? I feel bad for Derek."

Marty didn't answer at first, as if he was distracted. "Uh, yeah," he mumbled.

Jenn frowned. Why was Marty being so weird? She waited for him to say something else, but he just stared at the table.

She cleared her throat. "So, do you think the police have made any progress in tracking down the bike thief?"

Just then a kid screamed as another kid threw him into the water.

Marty jumped up. "Look, I gotta go." He rushed away toward the park entrance.

Jenn scratched her head. If she didn't know any better, she would think Marty was acting pretty nervous and suspicious. Why did he leave as soon as she mentioned the bike thief? Could he have really stolen that bike?!

Now, let me reveal the *real* reason Marty is so nervous. What Jenn doesn't know is that two months ago, at the start of summer, Marty came to this very park and he almost drowned while swimming with some friends. It was very traumatic for him and he hasn't been back to the park since. He doesn't like that he's let this fear of the water control him, so, when his cousin Jenn called that morning to ask if he'd meet her at the lake, he agreed. As soon as he agreed, he started to regret it. He got to the park and sat at a table waiting for Jenn. He started to feel sweaty and his hands were clammy. His heart beeat furiously inside his chest as the sounds of kids splashing brought back all the feelings of that day. Suddenly, he could almost feel himself going under and getting heavier and heavier. He felt dizzy with his swirling thoughts!

Then Jenn walked up. He tried to focus on what she was saying, but all he could hear was the splashing and screaming behind him. Suddenly, he jumped up. He had to get out of there and fast!

Now, go back and read the story excerpt again.

Do you see how knowing more about Marty's backstory completely changed how you saw him in the scene? He did have a secret and something he was hiding, which made him seem suspicious to Jenn. His secret wasn't that he had stolen the bike, like Jenn feared; his secret was that he was terrified of the water and of the lake.

The important takeaway is that parts of a character's history, even from long ago, can still affect how they act in the story today. If I were writing a timeline of this little scene, I would start with two months ago, when Marty almost drowned at the lake.

I would also include the fact that Marty had been saving for a bike, but was still far away from having enough money.

Marty's events on the timeline happen prior to the start of this story, but they're still very important to it. Because I created this past for Marty, when I write his scenes, I can use that secret history to make him a suspect in the story, and I can slowly reveal bits of his backstory as the case evolves. Some information I can use to make him seem more guilty, like the fact he was saving for a bike of his own and it wasn't going well. Other information I can use to clear his name, like the fact he was nervous because of being at the lake, not because he stole the bike.

You may be wondering what all this has to do with creating a timeline for your villain. Let me tell you! While backstory information is important for the suspects in your mystery, it is even more important for your villain. You need to get into the heart of why your villain is the way they are and why they have committed this particular crime. It is just as important as your detective's motives to solve the crime, if not more so!

Now this is the moment where you get to be really creative! Dig deep into your villain's heart/mind/and past. When was the first moment they decided to commit this crime? What is their past relationship with the victim like? Did they commit the crime in the heat of passion, or was there careful planning and preparations made? If they had to prepare things to pull off the crime, where do those events fall on your timeline?

Three Stages of a Crime

If you think of a crime in three stages (not to be confused with the three acts), it might help you in planning out your villain's actions.

1. Preparation Stage

This might be as simple as a growing hatred for the victim or as complicated as intricate plans made out over several days, weeks, or months. (This might happen before your story even starts.)

2. Committing the Crime

This will happen early in the first act, or even before. Did everything go as planned? Did anyone see them? Did they leave anything behind? What potential error could they have made that can lead to their capture later on?

3. "Clean up" Stage

This might mean the villain has to actively try to destroy evidence they forgot about, get rid of witnesses, or try to foil the detective's efforts to capture them. (This could happen throughout the three acts of your story.)

At every stage of your mystery, your villain should be actively trying to (1) plan the crime, (2) complete the crime, or (3) get away with the crime. So, if you don't know what your villain should be doing at any given moment, think about what "stage" of your story you are in, and you should get some ideas what your villain might be doing. In some stories your villain may not seem active in the "getting away with it" stage, but they might be laying low and trying to get away with the crime by staying out of sight and suspicion. That's okay too.

Start jotting down everything you know about the crime. Put in any and all events that involve your villain, starting with the past (before the crime), then moving into the present (what they were doing when the crime took place), and then into the future (what they did after the crime until the end of your book). If you don't know exactly what your villain is doing at a certain point, just leave it blank for now. You can always come back and fill it in at a later time, but really spend some time on this. The more you plan out the actions of your villain, the better your mystery story will be!

Remember to spend time on the physical props your villain used as well. What was the murder weapon? Where did your villain get it from, and when? What did they do with the murder weapon after the crime? Did they clean anything up or set things up to look differently than they really were? How did they get away?

Also, just like with a cat and a mouse, your detective and your villain will play off of each other. As one makes a choice, it forces the other to make a choice in reaction to or anticipation of the other's choices. As we fill out your villain's timeline, jot down new ideas that come to mind for how your hero might act or react.

Have you ever played in a symphonic band? If you did, you know that each instrument has their own piece of the music to play, called their "part." The oboes have one part, the flutes another, and so on. Things would get pretty messy fast if no one had the master plan, the music that had all the parts in one place. That is the "score" that the conductor has. It shows different lines for all the parts that are playing at one time. The conductor makes sure everyone comes in at the right time and that all the individual parts work together to make one harmonious musical experience for the audience.

You're like a conductor when you write a novel. A mystery novel, in particular, has many different parts to it and they all need to come in at just the right moment. So, how do you keep from getting confused? Just like the conductor has their score, you have your timeline. After you create your timeline, you can figure out where it falls within the three Acts of your story. It may sound confusing, but let's look at an example to get a better idea.

The next page is a villain timeline made from a Scooby-Doo episode ("Decoy for a Dognapper" from the original *Scooby-Doo, Where Are You*!). It shows the villain's movements and his motivation for committing the crime.

Villain: Buck Masters Timeline and Movements

Initial Plan and Motivation

Motivation: Buck Masters wants his dog, Duchess, to win the grand prize at dog shows.

Plan: To ensure Duchess wins, Buck decides to kidnap other prize-winning dogs to eliminate the competition.

First Set of Dognappings

Action: Buck kidnaps several prize-winning dogs in the area.

Movement: He discreetly abducts these dogs and hides them in a secret location, away from public view.

Suspicion Arises

Action: The disappearance of multiple prize-winning dogs raises suspicion among the dog owners and the authorities.

Movement: Buck notices the increasing suspicion and realises he needs to divert attention away from himself.

Staging Duchess's Kidnapping

Action: To deflect suspicion, Buck stages the kidnapping of his own dog, Duchess.

Movement: He carefully plans and executes the fake abduction, ensuring it looks like Duchess is also a victim of the dognapper.

Scooby-Doo and the Gang's Involvement

Action: The Scooby-Doo gang sets up Scooby as bait to catch the dognapper.

Movement: Buck falls for the trap and dognaps Scooby, thinking he's another prize-winning dog.

Hideout Activities

Action: Buck takes Scooby and the other kidnapped dogs to his hideout, evading the Scooby gang.

Movement: He frequently visits the hideout to check on the dogs and maintain their captivity.

Final Confrontation

Action: Buck accidentally leaves some clues and inadvertently leads the Scooby-Doo gang to his hideout.

Movement: During the final confrontation, Buck tries to escape but is eventually caught by the gang and the authorities.

Revelation and Capture

Action: Buck's plan is revealed by the Scooby-Doo gang, exposing his motive and the staged kidnapping of Duchess.

Movement: Buck is captured and taken into custody, ending his dognapping scheme.

By creating a timeline with all the events of the crime, you are able to see a "master plan" of the crime. Take a moment and write out the main events of your crime and the main movements of your villain. Figure out where on the timeline the crime should go, and then work backwards and forwards moving out from it.

After you have created it, try placing your timeline over your three-acts and the plot worksheet you made earlier. This will help you to see where all the events of your story fit within the story beats, chapters, and acts.

In the next pages, you'll see that I've included Buck Masters's villain timeline over the three-act story structure of the Scooby-Doo episode.

TIP

Think of a villain timeline as your secret cheat sheet. By mapping out their every move and scheme, you keep their actions in check and ensure their plans make sense. This way, you avoid any plot holes and keep your mystery tight and thrilling, with every twist and turn perfectly timed.

ACT 1
The Beginning

Introduce your characters and get the story started!

ACT 2
PART ONE
The Middle

The hero decides to go for it but soon realises things are harder than they seem.

Opening	A series of prize-winning dogs have been kidnapped.
Inciting Incident	Scooby-Doo and the gang learn about the recent dognappings and decide to investigate.
Setup	The gang discovers that the dognappings are part of a larger pattern and suspect foul play.
Call to Action	The gang decides to use Scooby as bait to catch the dognapper.
The Choice	The gang disguises Scooby to attract the dognapper and plan to follow him.
Try/Fail	The Villain falls for the trap and kidnaps Scooby.
Midpoint	The gang follows the Villain to his hideout.

Buck Masters starts kidnapping dogs.

Buck begins to sense that the authorities are closing in on him.

Buck decides to stage the kidnapping of his own dog, Duchess, to divert suspicion away from himself.

Buck takes the bait and kidnaps Scooby-Doo.

Buck take Scooby back to his hideout.

Buck Masters plans to kidnap prize-winning dogs to eliminate competition for his showdog, Duchess.

ACT 2

PART TWO

The Middle

The villain almost crushes the hero, who starts to lose hope. But wait...

ACT 3

The End

The hero comes up with a plan that turns things around. And...VICTORY!

Stage	Above the timeline	Below the timeline
Rising Threats	The gang discovers the hideout, but the Villain gets away with the kidnapped dogs!	Buck escapes through the vents before the Scooby gang can catch him.
Dark Moment	The gang plans their next step, but the Villain escapes again.	Buck successfully evades the gang a second time.
		Buck hides with his remaining kidnapped dogs.
Turning Point	The gang re-evaluates their approach, realising the Villain has been using the vents to evade them.	
A New Plan	The gang uses their new information to devise a new plan.	
		Buck tries to escape through the vents again but is unsuccessful as the gang outsmarts him.
Climax	There's a dramatic confrontation at the hideout. They manage to rescue Scooby and the other kidnapped dogs, and capture the Villain.	
Resolution	Buck Masters' scheme is exposed, and he is taken into custody.	

For your timeline, you can create a template like this and fill it in, or take out a piece of paper and draw it out. It can go up and down, or side to side. The point of drawing your timeline is to get a visual idea of where the events of your story fall and what the main characters—the villain and the detective—are doing. This is why we recommend creating a chart.

For example, imagine your villain steels a rare coin. Since the villain owns an antique shop, they stash it among their collection of rare artifacts. The villain's action of hiding the stolen coin would have its own line on the timeline graph. The readers don't know they did this—it's not part of the story beats.

Later in the story, the young detective, a 12-year-old girl who first noticed her elderly neighbour's rare coin missing from his collection, starts to suspect the villain. The neighbour had recently mentioned that the stolen coin had a distinctive engraving of a historic landmark. Suspecting that the coin might be at the antique shop, the detective carefully investigates.

During her search, she discovers a coin display in the shop's back room. Among the many old pieces, she finds the missing coin—bearing the exact engraving described by her neighbour—alongside other antiques. This discovery is marked as a key clue on the timeline, showing her breakthrough in solving the case. The readers see her finding the coin, and the discovery is part of an action beat (maybe the Turning Point or the Climax).

Just like with all of your writing, your timeline can change as your story develops. This means nothing about your writing, including the timeline, is permanent. So, don't sweat if you don't know exactly what things should happen or the order of it all. Just start playing around with creating a timeline of the major events that you know will happen in your book. Take a look at the plot you created earlier. You know that your story needs to include most of these story beats, but remember, these aren't the only things that happen in your story.

TIP

To make it easier to overlay your villain's timeline with your story beats, try colour-coding or using visual markers for key events. This way, you can quickly see how the villain's actions align with or affect the plot, ensuring that every twist and turn fits perfectly into your mystery's overall structure.

STEP 8

Plan the Hero's Timeline

Your hero's journey is about to kick off! As you plan their timeline, think about how they'll react to the villain's moves. It's a cat-and-mouse game, and your hero is on the trail. Plan it out and let the chase begin!

STEP 8

Plan the Hero's Timeline

Creating Your Hero's Timeline

IF THE HERO is the protagonist of your story, and they appear in nearly all the scenes, why do you need a timeline for them? Isn't the plot outline basically the hero's timeline?

Is that what you're asking? Those are good questions! Here's the answer:

The plot outline shows the big picture, while the hero's timeline shows a more focused view of the hero.

Not only does the hero's timeline help focus on the protagonist's personal journey and growth, it zeroes in on their specific actions, decisions, and emotions. AND, by integrating the hero's timeline with the villain's timeline you create a more exciting and dynamic story. It gives you the framework to show a clear interplay between the hero's and villain's actions.

Villains, be afraid! The detective is here to ensure justice is served and that no one gets away with murder.

In creating your hero's timeline, the first thing to decide is when you want your detective to first come onto the scene. You basically have two options: before the crime, or after the crime.

If you choose before the crime, how do you want to first introduce your main character? Will they meet the victim before the crime takes place? Think about a fun way to introduce your detective into the story.

If you choose after the crime, the most popular way to bring your detective onto the scene is with the discovery of the crime or as the initial investigation is underway.

Thinking about what genre, or kind, of mystery story you are writing can help with this decision. Many cozy mysteries have amateur detectives who either have some personal connection to the case or have some reason for getting involved in it, such as discovering a body or overhearing or seeing something they weren't meant to see. If this is your type of story, think of reasons that your detective might be thrown into the path of the crime.

If you are writing a police procedural, many of these start with a new detective joining the department or we meet the detective as they come onto the scene to investigate the crime. Knowing what kind of story you are writing can help you decide some of these choices about when and how to introduce your detective to the story.

Another question to ask is why—why is your detective drawn to *this* case? Again, if this is a police story, the simple answer might be your detective was assigned to the case. If this is a cozy mystery and your detective is a fifteen-year-old kid, you'll need to come up with a believable reason for your detective to get involved in solving the crime. Sometimes the relationships your detective has can help put them into unusual situations, such as going to visit a grandma or aunt for the summer in a tiny little town where the crime takes place. You might even try a "locked room" mystery where the characters literally can't leave a place and your detective is committed to solving the crime just so they can go home!

After the initial crime scene discovery/investigation, what kinds of things should your detective do? Just think about the kinds of things you would do if you were trying to solve a mystery. You might talk to people who have information you need, such as experts. You would definitely want to interview people who have firsthand knowledge of what happened or who were there, such as witnesses. You would want to question any "persons of interest" or suspects you had in mind as you gather information and clues. Your detective would do the same kind of things.

Here are some ideas for timeline events you can add to the detective's timeline:

Possible Timeline Events for Your Detective

First Clue Discovered: The detective finds an important clue at the crime scene.

Interview with a Key Witness: The detective talks to someone who might have seen or heard something crucial.

Suspect Interrogation: The detective questions a suspect, who may or may not be telling the truth.

Unexpected Challenge: The detective faces a setback, like a lost clue or a suspect giving false information.

New Evidence Uncovered: The detective uncovers new evidence that points in a different direction.

Following a Lead: The detective follows a promising lead, which could either help or mislead them.

Partner or Ally Assistance: The detective gets help from a partner, friend, or unexpected ally.

Personal Conflict: The detective deals with a personal issue that distracts them from the case.

Close Call with Danger: The detective has a narrow escape from a dangerous situation.

Clue Fits into Place: A previously confusing clue suddenly makes sense, bringing the detective closer to solving the case.

Can you think of any others?

Discovery of a Motive: The detective uncovers a suspect's motive for the crime.

Surprise Twist: The detective encounters a twist that changes their understanding of the case.

Confrontation with the Villain: The detective confronts the villain or someone they suspect strongly.

False Accusation: The detective accuses someone who turns out to be innocent.

Villain's Mistake: The detective notices a small mistake the villain made, leading to a breakthrough.

Hidden Clue Revealed: A clue hidden in plain sight is finally noticed by the detective.

Race Against Time: The detective realises they're running out of time to solve the case.

Trap for the Villain: The detective sets a trap to catch the villain.

Final Piece of the Puzzle: The detective puts together the last piece of the puzzle, revealing the villain's identity.

The Arrest: The detective confronts and catches the villain, solving the case.

As your detective moves throughout their timeline, pay attention to your villain's timeline. Think about how you can keep your villain just one step ahead of your detective, until the end when all is revealed. How can your villain mess up and interfere with your detective and their investigation? Remember, your detective is the hero of your story. We like stories where heroes have to overcome hard things and earn their right to a happy ending. Success that comes too easily will fall flat and won't excite your readers.

So, think of ways you can use your villain and the circumstances of your story to actively work against your detective on their journey to discovering the truth. Give your detective false starts, trails that run cold, and dead ends. Let us see your detective be confused, discouraged, and unsure of themself. But, of course, don't stop there! Your detective must always pick themself back up again and keep going. Let their perseverance frustrate the villain. Give your story a hero that your audience can root for who doesn't give up when the going gets tough.

As you plan your hero's movements on their timeline, always keep in mind *where* in the story you are, as in, which Act of the story the action takes place within. For instance, you already know the kinds of things that should happen in Act 1. All you have to do is look at the story beats.

If you are in Act 2 near the middle, you know the Midpoint story beat will be happening—the revelation of new information that sends your story (and investigation) into a new direction. If you are ever feeling stuck or like you don't know what should happen next, just pull out your outline or plot worksheet. This is why we put so much work into figuring out the story beforehand. It is super helpful to have these items at your fingertips when you find yourself in the middle of your novel and you aren't sure where to go next.

So, are you ready to take a stab at your own hero timeline?

Just make sure you don't literally stab anyone or anything, okay?

Good.

TIP

To intertwine the villain and hero timelines, think of it like a dance: each step the villain takes should lead the hero to the next move. Make sure their actions and reactions sync up perfectly, creating a thrilling tango of twists and turns. This way, both timelines will waltz together, keeping your readers on their toes!

How to Add the Hero's Timeline to the Plot Outline

Identify Key Events
Start with your plot outline and identify the major story beats and events. Note where the hero is involved in these moments.

Create Parallel Tracks
In your plot outline, create a parallel track specifically for the hero's timeline. This track will run alongside your main plot events.

Map the Hero's Actions and Reactions
For each major plot point, detail the hero's actions and emotional responses. This will capture their personal journey and how they are impacted by the events.

Highlight Character Development
Make note of key moments that contribute to the hero's growth and development. This might include overcoming a personal challenge or forming relationships.

React to the Villain's Timeline
Ensure that the hero's actions and decisions are in response to the villain's moves. This keeps the hero's timeline dynamic and intertwined with the villain's plans, showing how the hero is constantly reacting to and countering the villain.

Turn the page and have a look at the the plot outline for *The Lion King*. In this example, I've laid out the timelines for both Simba and Scar, so you can see how the hero and villain's journeys unfold side by side. These timelines will give you a clear idea of how their actions, choices, and pivotal moments are woven together to create the story's tension and drama. Take a close look to see how the timelines intersect, overlap, and diverge—this will give you a strong visual of what your own story's outline might look like when the hero and villain are in play.

TIP

Charting timelines and acts can be like trying to juggle flaming torches—without a plan, things might get messy! To make it easier, start by mapping out each act and timeline separately, then overlay them like puzzle pieces. This way, you'll see how each part fits together and ensure nothing gets dropped along the way. It's all about keeping the fire under control and the plot moving smoothly!

Opening

Simba, the newborn lion cub, to the Pride Lands by his father, King Mufasa.

Inciting Incident

Scar, Mufasa's brother, becomes envious of Simba's future role as king and begins plotting to usurp the throne.

Setup

Simba grows up, learns about the circle of life, and the dangers beyond the Pride Lands.

Call to Action

Scar orchestrates a wildebeest stampede to kill Simba and Mufasa. Mufasa dies saving Simba.

The Choice

Simba, overwhelmed with guilt, decides to leave the Pride Lands and runs away.

Try/Fail

Simba lives a carefree life in the jungle with Timon and Pumbaa, avoiding responsibility.

Midpoint

Nala, Simba's childhood friend, finds him and tells him that Scar has ruined the Pride Lands. She urges his return.

Scar's bitterness and sense of entitlement fuel his desire for power. He begins plotting to overthrow Mufasa and Simba.

Scar manipulates the hyenas, convincing them to align with him.

Scar makes a plan to kill Mufasa and Simba. His control over the hyenas is crucial in executing his plan.

Scar seizes control of the Pride Lands, enforces his rule, and aligns himself with the hyenas. He uses them as enforcers to instill fear in the lions.

Scar makes poor decisions regarding hunting and dismisses any concerns from other lions.

Simba learns from Mufasa and explores the Pride Lands. He is carefree and curious.

Simba's desire to prove that he's brave leads him into danger, highlighting his innocence and desire to impress his father.

Simba's decision to run away is driven by guilt and fear, marking a shift in his character.

Simba struggles with his guilt and his attempt to escape his past leads to stagnation in his development.

Simba deals with an internal struggle and realises he can't run from who he is.

The plot outline of The Lion King with the Hero Timeline (left) and the Villain Timeline (right)

Rising Threats

Simba returns to the Pride Lands.
He confronts Scar and battles his hyenas.

After the initial confrontation, Simba is initially defeated and forced to retreat, regrouping with his allies.

Dark Moment

Simba doubts his ability to defeat Scar and restore order.
He struggles with the weight of his past mistakes.

Turning Point

Simba receives guidance from the spirit of Mufasa, who reminds him of his place as king.

A New Plan

Simba and his friends devise a new plan to defeat Scar.
They rally the animals to their cause.

Climax

With the help of his allies, Simba defeats Scar and restores order to the Pride Lands.

Resolution

Simba is crowned king, the Pride Lands are restored to their former glory, and peace is returned.

Scar's paranoia grows as he realises the consequences of his actions, leading to a more oppressive and desperate reign.

Scar uses fear and intimidation to suppress dissent, but his grip on power begins to weaken as he loses the loyalty of both the pride and the hyenas.

Scar tries to blame Mufasa's death on the hyenas.

Scar is defeated by Simba and is killed by the hyenas for betraying them.

The vision of Mufasa helps Simba deal with his internal struggle.

Simba's new sense of duty and his desire to restore balance marks his growth into the role of a leader.

The battle represents Simba's acceptance of his identity and his role as the rightful king,

Simba becomes the King Mufasa always knew he could be.

STEP 9

Bury the Clues and Plant the Red Herrings

Here's where the fun really starts! Hide your clues carefully and toss in a few distractions. The more subtle you are, the more satisfying the reveal will be. It's all part of crafting a mystery that keeps readers guessing until the very end.

STEP 9

Bury the Clues and Plant the Red Herrings

Tricks, Twists, and Hidden Tips

YOU MAY BE WONDERING just how your detective is going to possibly figure everything out, and how you are going to plan it!

Actually, it doesn't have to be as hard as it sounds. Since you are creating this story, you get to *create* the clues that your detective will follow as they trace the villain and try to catch them. Remember the story of Hansel and Gretel, and how Hansel leaves little pieces of bread behind himself to find his way back out of the forest? Just pretend that your villain is dropping little clues along the way that your detective will find. Of course, your villain doesn't *mean* to leave clues, and they don't do it on purpose. But since they aren't perfect, their little mistakes leave a trail that your clever sleuth will be able to follow.

This chapter will outline how to insert clues into your story, and how to keep them hidden and yet still believable when your detective discovers them. Remember, your ultimate job is to bring your readers to the end of the mystery and to try to keep them guessing right up to the end. They should get to the end and think, "Gee, I should've seen that coming," and yet still not see it coming. That is your goal, for it to feel believable and yet still be a surprise.

You will do this through the use of clues. Clues have two jobs: to lead your readers to the solution of the mystery, and to keep your readers from getting there. It's kind of like laying out a path for someone to follow, and then purposefully leaving holes that they will stumble into along the way. I know, it's kind of mean, but you want to be a mystery writer, right? It's not for the faint of heart!

Here are some tried and true tricks to plant clues in the story, but still keep them on the down low:

TIP

Planting clues is like hiding treasure—just make sure your readers can find it without needing a map! Drop hints and pieces of evidence throughout your story in a way that feels natural, but don't make it too obvious. Subtlety is key: you want readers to be intrigued, not hit over the head with a clue-by-four. Think of it as leading them on a treasure hunt where the prize is solving your mystery!

Show a Real Clue, Then a Fake One

If you show a real clue first, like mud on someone's boots, immediately go on to another "clue" or detail that actually doesn't mean anything. Your reader's will focus on the last clue and let the first one slip by.

Shine the Spotlight on the Wrong Thing

This is similar to the last one, but a little different. Show your clue, say the fact that the victim gets her hair done every Wednesday at the salon, but shine the spotlight on an unimportant part of the clue instead of the real thing. For instance, let's say the important detail about the clue is that the victim gets her hair done every week, at the same time, and the killer knows that, so they used the time to set the stage for the murder later in the day. You might distract from that part of the clue by emphasising which hairdresser the victim always sees, or some other unimportant detail to throw your readers off the track.

Clues With No Context

This means, show clues early on before there is even a crime at all to tie any special meaning to the clue. Who cares that the granny in the story is also a weightlifter! Early on, it doesn't mean anything and will come across as just a quirky character trait. But later, when the body is moved to a new location, you will need granny to be strong enough to do it. Because you mentioned the info early on, no one will really connect the dots. We hope!

Let your Detective Make Mistakes

Let your detective see a clue, but not realise it is important. By doing this, you introduce the clue but because the detective didn't care about it (at least at the time), your audience will blow right past it as well.

The Clue that Never Was

This is where the "clue" is actually the thing that is missing. Pretty clever, huh? For example, if everyone at a concert received a hand stamp, and the villain claims they attended but doesn't have the stamp, that would be a clue that they are lying.

A Little Bit at a Time

This technique is where you reveal a part of a clue at a time, spread out over the story. Maybe you show a muddy bicycle track, but no bike, and no reason for that to be important until you later show that the robbery happened on a rainy night with lots of mud.

Right in Front of Your Nose

Have you ever looked and looked for something only to later find it was sitting right there in plain sight all the time? Sometimes, *not* hiding the clue can actually help it to disappear and seem unimportant. Your readers won't notice the clue, because they are too busy trying to find what is hidden.

Shiny, Flashy Lights

Distraction is key to pulling things over on people. Think about a magician! They have sequined shiny capes, coloured lights, flashy music, maybe even rabbits and doves. The point? If you are looking at all the shiny/flashy things, you won't see them pull off the trick right in front of you. Can you add some drama, maybe an argument, that actually has nothing to do with your plot? Try to throw in something exciting, like an escaped prisoner, so that no one suspects the weightlifting granny.

Time (It's On My Side)

Give your villain an air-tight alibi. There is no way they could be the suspect because they were teaching a class when the murder occurred. They were seen by over 30 students! Later on, you can reveal that the crime actually happened at a different time (and reveal how the villain fooled everyone into thinking something different). Or you can show how the villain actually slipped out from where they were and was able to commit the crime all along. In our teacher example, maybe the teacher *was* teaching a class, but they failed to say it was student presentation day and that the students were showing their films all class period in the dark room. That's a perfect opportunity to leave unnoticed.

Disguise Your Clues With a Skirmish

Let's say your detective is poking around an empty warehouse. They notice a rope tied to the upper beam, but before they can investigate further (and before the readers can realise the rope is important), someone clobbers the detective on the head with an empty bottle. The next scene is them waking up inside a trunk!

By showing the rope right before a dangerous or active scene, you steal any thunder the clue has and force the readers to pay attention to the current danger your detective is in.

TIP

Clues should be like breadcrumbs leading your readers through the story. Make sure each clue serves a purpose and ties back to the main plot. Avoid making them too obvious, but also ensure they're not so obscure that they frustrate your readers. A good clue should be just challenging enough to be rewarding when discovered.

Three Kinds of Clues

Remember, clues can come in all kinds of shapes and sizes. Here are the top three kinds.

Physical

A clue may be something physical, like a fingerprint, a glove, broken glass, a pearl from a necklace, or a crumpled paper.

Verbal

A clue can be verbal, such as a character mentioning they are in debt (revealing why someone might have a motive), or expressing their hidden feelings of anger toward the victim. These kinds of clues obviously show up in dialogue as your detective conducts interviews with suspects and witnesses.

Thematic

A clue can also be thematic. For instance, the mere fact a particular character is pale, thin, and has a devious laugh makes them suspicious. You can use your readers' previous experiences and assumptions to either confirm what you want them to suspect about someone (that they are bad), or to lead them astray (by making someone who is actually good *appear* to be bad).

Where are places that these kinds of clues might hide? Verbal clues can show up in dialogue as characters talk to, and interview, one another ("But Aunt Margo didn't come to tea yesterday. It was very unusual for her to miss it"). Thematic clues might show up in the kind of weather (a dark and stormy night), or the way a setting is described (a dark and unfriendly room). Physical clues can show up in your setting as well, like the discovery of a secret passageway leading from the gym storage closet to the cafeteria.

Red Herrings

The term "Red Herring" means a false clue meant to distract and throw someone (like your readers) off the path. A herring is a kind of fish and in the 1800s, preserved/cured herring (which turn bright red) were used in foxhunting. If your hounds were too good, they would find the fox right off and the hunt wouldn't be much of hunt after all. So, some hunters came up with the idea of using red herring, which are very smelly, to distract the hounds from the scent of the fox. They would drag these smelly fish across the path. I imagine, to a hound, a smelly fish is quite enticing.

What do mystery writers mean when we use the term red herring? Are you supposed to throw dried fish at your readers? Well, not exactly, but kind of. A red herring has come to mean a false clue meant to confuse and muddle your readers so that the hunt (to find out whodunnit) doesn't become too easy. Just like hunters don't like a fox hunt that lasts ten minutes, no one likes a mystery that is easy to figure out.

When creating red herrings, think about your suspects, for starters. Can you give each of them a few red herrings? What kind of fake clue might make that individual seem more suspicious?

One thing to remember, a red herring must become obvious in the course of the story that it was a false clue. Before you end the story, you must show how each major red herring wasn't a *real* clue after all. If you don't do this, the actual path to your villain will get muddled and confusing. You don't want readers finishing your book and thinking, "But what about the cab driver and the gun? Did that have something to do with it or not?" Just remember, you need to resolve the major red herrings, but little ones that are easily forgotten or dropped as the story moves forward? Don't worry about them.

So, how exactly do you create red herrings in your story? Here are a few tips to get you started:

Make Your Characters Mysterious

Remember, a red herring is supposed to lead people away from the real villain and throw suspicion onto others. The more secrets you have in your book, the better. Not all the secrets have to be devious ones but giving people something to hide will naturally make them more suspicious. Then you can plant red herrings about the secrets, which all have nothing to do with the actual crime.

Give Your Characters a Reason to Hide Their Mystery

Okay, so the shifty-eyed, pizza delivery-driver who brings you your Friday night double pepperoni is also a black belt in martial arts. Why does that have to be a secret? Maybe they're hiding from someone dangerous or trying to start a new life where no one knows their past. Make sure your characters have stakes and something to lose if their secret gets out. The more they have to protect, the more tension and intrigue you'll build in your story. Why do they care so much to protect their secret? And how far will they go to keep it hidden?

Don’t Make Your Red Herrings *TOO* Good

Nobody likes a show-off. You want to distract your readers, but you don’t want to make it impossible for them to guess the identity of your true villain. If you don’t have any clues pointing to your real villain until just before the end, that isn’t very fair, right? Just make sure you are laying enough real clues as well as red herrings so that your audience doesn’t get mad.

Don’t Worry About Red Herrings Until You Have a Solid Story Written Out

If a false clue comes to you as you’re writing, throw it in, but for the most part, red herrings can be added in after you’ve written out your story. That means, figure out the main story, work from your timelines, and don’t worry too much about red herrings and false clues until you have that down first.

If you still feel unsure about red herrings, don’t overthink it. A red herring can be someone who seems shady, but really isn’t. Or it can be an object or event that appears to be important, but actually doesn’t matter much to the plot at all. It can even be something intentionally planted by your villain meant to lead everyone astray. Who better to plant to a red herring than the villain themself!

The bottom line is this: clues and red herrings are nothing to stress over. Get your story down first and the clues and red herrings will be easier to make up afterward.

Now, are you ready to learn about the part of your story your whole book is building toward? That's right, it's time to talk about the big reveal!

TIP

When planting red herrings, remember they're meant to mislead, not confuse. Place them strategically where they can divert attention without disrupting the flow of the story. Just like a magician's trick, your red herrings should keep readers guessing but should never overshadow the real clues.

STEP 10

Unravel the Mystery

This is it—the moment of truth! All your hard work pays off as your hero cracks the case. Make sure your big reveal ties everything together in a way that surprises and delights your readers. They won't see it coming!

STEP 10

Unravel the Mystery

The Big Reveal

AFTER GETTING TO THE END of a mystery, nothing is better than a good reveal. The reveal is the climactic scene of the story, the moment we finally get to know whodunnit!

We've followed the investigation from the first hint of crime. We've trailed after suspects and hunted down clues. We've even followed a few red herrings. We've watched our detective get insights (Eureka!) and watched their disappointment as the trail ran cold. But now, we know we're close. Everything has built up and led to this moment, and we're ready!

The reveal, or the moment your detective reveals how the crime was done and whodunnit, is the payoff your readers get for following along on the mystery adventure. After all their work, and yours, you want to make sure to give them the best reveal scene you can. This is not time for rushing to the end.

As you approach this point, it's crucial to increase the challenges your detective faces. Create situations that make the reader question whether the detective can succeed. The more obstacles you present, the more satisfying it will be when they triumph over adversity. Consider making your detective doubt their own abilities as well. After all, even the best detectives have their "I can't believe I missed that!" moments. By intensifying both external conflicts and internal struggles, you'll ensure that the tension rises steadily to a breaking point.

Remember, the climax is where all the conflict in the novel reaches a boiling point. After all, you can't have two people fighting desperately for opposite things and not have it result in a showdown.

I know what you may be thinking. "But my story is a mystery, not a superhero story. It doesn't have two people fighting desperately for opposite things!"

Are you sure? Think about it! You have a villain who wants nothing more than to get away with their crime. You also have a detective who wants nothing more than to catch the person who committed the crime. That sounds like the makings of a pretty good showdown to me!

Of course, the kind of climactic scene you have might depend on the genre of mystery you are writing. If your story is dark and gritty, like a noir or a police procedural, you might have a showdown that literally has your detective's life at stake. But, if your story is a cozy mystery, or perhaps a quirky lockdown set in a high school, your showdown might have more to do with setting a trap to catch the crook in some situation that forces them to prove their guilt. Either way, it will be exciting!

So, how do you create a reveal that will meet all your reader's hopes and dreams? A good reveal should include three things:

1 - Who committed the crime
2 - How they did it (means)
3 - Why they did it (motive)
4 - When they did it (opportunity)
5 - How your detective figured it all out

Once your villain is caught and all the danger (or danger of escape) is over, that is the time for the reveal. Your detective will set out to explain just how the villain was able to commit the crime and where they went wrong. In other words, you definitely want to include how your detective was able to solve the case. This is your detective's time to shine! If your readers have already solved the case, they will be happy to know they were right and enjoy seeing if the clues they saw are the same as your detective's clues. If your readers were not able to solve the crime, they will be excited to finally find out who did it. They will also enjoy seeing how clever the detective was to be able to catch such a devious crook.

This is, above all, the time to make sure you are playing fair. Here's what that means:

Imagine you are reading my story. You have followed the detective along paying attention to clues, avoiding red herrings. Everything seems to be pointing to the toymaker with the grudge against Mr Kringle, the man who plays Santa every year in the big parade. But then, at the big reveal, your detective suddenly reveals that the grumpy toymaker was actually out of town when Mr Kringle's Santa suit was stolen. Nobody up to this point has given any hint that the toymaker was out of town. But your detective suddenly knows this because of checking the train records for the week of the crime (something that was also left out of the book). The actual Santa suit thief? It was the jealous Mr Hinkle, who only ever gets to play the Easter Bunny.

Do you see how this isn't playing fair? How could you possibly know that the toymaker was out of town if you weren't given any of that information in the book? Pulling out secret info at the last minute is a sure-fire way to make your mystery readers mad. Don't do it!

After you have written your climactic reveal scene, make sure all the clues make sense. Would your detective *really* be able to piece everything together with the clues you offered? If the answer is yes, great! If the answer is no, don't despair. You can still go back and add in clues that you find are missing. That is the great thing about writing. You don't have to do it in order. If you're at the end of your story and find that you forgot to put a detail in at the beginning, just go ahead and add it in.

So, now you know how to create a reveal scene that will delight your readers. Just be careful! You're liable to make fans that will want you to get right to work on that next book.

Up next, all you need to know about getting your book ready for readers.

That's right, we're going to talk about editing and revising to take what you've written and make it shine.

STEP 11

Write, Revise, and Refine

Your story is almost there! Writing is just the first part; now it's time to polish your masterpiece. Go through your work with a keen eye, refining sentences, tightening your plot, and making sure every word counts. This step might take a bit of time, but it's where your story truly shines. Keep pushing forward—you're almost done!

STEP 11

Write
Revise
Refine

Polishing Your Masterpiece

IF YOU'RE READING this, it probably means you have finished your novel. Hooray! I'm so proud of you and all the work you put into your book!

Of course, if you're reading this it might mean you're the kind of person who likes to get all the information first before starting. That's great too! This chapter will be full of useful information for when you get to the end of your book.

Do you know how many people finish the novels they set out to write, let alone how many kids? Not many! Take a moment to pat yourself on the back and let it sink in. You, my friend, have written a book. That is pretty amazing.

Finishing your story can feel so amazing that often writers are tempted to print the whole thing out and hand it out to everyone they know. That would be a mistake.

Until your book has been edited and revised, it is still a first draft. Editing means to look for ways the story can be stronger. Revising means to make the changes that need to be made. What do I mean by a first draft? A first draft is the version you have of your story when you have finished writing it out for the first time. A first draft doesn't mean it's bad, especially if you have worked out a plot and timelimes to begin with; it just means it's not finished.

Now, here's the hard part. Your wonderful mystery story that you have created still needs work to be a finished book. Sometimes that can be very disappointing to realise. Sometimes we just want to be done! Don't worry—you'll be done, and sooner than you think, but first you owe your awesome story the chance to be the best it can be. You've put too much work into it to just slap it together now.

Your first draft served a special job. It was the first time you ever let this story become an actual story, not just an idea. Hopefully, you let your imagination go and you came up with ideas that even surprised you. It can be a lot of fun. This is the stage where you let your creativity run free.

But now it is time to start editing and revising this first draft into a second draft. Your second draft is where you take off the writer's hat and put on the editor's cap. It is time to read your story and look clearly at what works and what doesn't. There may be parts, characters, scenes that kind of stick out. They don't really fit with what your story became. They may need to be cut. There may be other areas that feel promising, but you didn't stop to explore them at the time. These areas might need more, and you may want to go back and see what you want to add.

Make no mistake, revising is hard work! Sometimes you really love a part of your book, but you know deep in your heart that your travelling umbrella salesperson just doesn't fit anywhere in the book. You have to have a cool, keen eye and a steady hand like a surgeon. If you know the salesperson doesn't belong, they must be cut. Everything must work together for the good of the story, no matter how hard it can seem.

But don't be discouraged! I have compiled a list of my top three editing and revising tips on the next page.

TIP

Editing your manuscript is like giving your story a fresh haircut—sometimes, it's all about trimming the excess and highlighting the best features. After your first draft, take a step back, read through your work with fresh eyes, and be ready to cut out the fluff, tighten the plot, and polish your characters.

Stay Positive

We all want to believe we're secret geniuses who can whip out an amazing, perfect book in one pass, and we can feel bad when we realise the book we wrote still needs some work. But the truth is, every writer has to revise. From Shakespeare to Lemony Snicket, writers don't automatically create masterpieces from the get-go. They write, then edit, then revise. And you should, too!

Make Cuts Like Your Book Depends On It

Cutting out things that weigh your book down is one way to instantly make your story better. Do you have random subplots that don't really work, too many side characters, dialogue that drags on, or clunky boring descriptions? Cut! Do you use three words when one word could work? Cut! As you read your book, look for places where you feel bored or distracted. Chances are these areas can be cut or at least pared down.

Start Big and Work Toward Small

When it comes to edits and revisions, always look at the big picture first. Sure, you could spend an hour making the dialogue of a scene really shine, but what if you decide the whole scene needs to go? All that work will be for nothing. (Well, not really, because all writing and editing practice just helps you get better!) First read the whole book, get a feel for the areas you want to keep, cut, or change. After you make big edits, you can focus on the smaller ones like your word choice and your dialogue.

So, there you go. Some top tips to start your editing process. But let's dive a little deeper into how to look at the big picture of your story. Get out your plot worksheet. Did the story you write follow your original plot? Change isn't bad, but just make sure the changes you made still fit with your master plan for your book. You want a book that is balanced and keeps most of the story beats of great storytelling.

As you hold your story up to your plot, you may realise that a scene or chapter you wrote would be better some place else. That is totally okay! This is the time for big changes. You may want to set your first plot aside and create a new plot worksheet for the story you actually wrote (your first draft). This can be helpful to see if there are any plot holes or things you meant to include but you left out. It's easy to fix these areas once you know where they are.

Take a look at your opening. It's normal to need a whole new opening after you get to the end of your book. Sometimes, the place doesn't really match up with the place we ended up. And that's okay, too! Maybe you started your story thinking you would write about a kid who uncovers a plot to steal the crown jewels, but you ended up writing a story about a kid who discovers a plot to murder the King. Just write a new opening that better sets up the story you ended up writing.

Once your big picture edits are done and you've made the revisions, you have your second draft.

Surely, your second draft is now ready to be printed or published, right?

Um, not quite.

It's time to jump into your third draft.

In this draft, you will get to finally get into the nitty-gritty of your book. Remember that boring dialogue you've been itching to fix? Now is the time! Cut out most filler words—that, really, seemed, very, kind of. Pare down descriptions that go on and on. What is the best word of the five you used to describe the knife? Use that one.

Take a look at your verbs next. Are they active and precise? Are you saying, "He walked," when you could say "He strutted" through the room? See what I mean? Use your verbs to add life to your characters and the choices they make.

When you've finished this round of edits and revisions, listen to your book out loud. You can read your book out loud, or you can have a word processor read it for you like Microsoft Word or Google Docs. It will sound a little like a computer or robot reading it (because it is), but there is no substitute for hearing your words read aloud. It is the best way to catch little mistakes and clunky passages.

Pay attention to your dialogue. Does it sound like how real people talk? If it doesn't, how can you fix it? Last of all, run your book through a spellcheck and make sure you are using the right form of commonly mistaken words, such as their, there, and they're.

Once you've done all this, congratulations! You have a polished third draft that's ready for test readers! These "test" readers are called "Beta readers" and they are super helpful as you improve your story.

Beta readers are the first audience for your book. Their job is to give you feedback on the story. Was something confusing?

Did they get lost or miss an important detail about your crime so that your reveal fell flat? Having their honest feedback is very helpful as you improve your story.

How should you pick your beta readers? Ideally, they are people who like you and like the kinds of stories you like. Your parents are good candidates. Maybe even your brother or sister or cousin. I bet you know a couple of friends who would like to read your story. If someone says they'd rather not read it, don't fret too much. For some people, reading just isn't their thing, and that's okay too. Just try to find anywhere from two to five people who can read your book and give you some thoughts about it. Ask them to look for places they felt confused or bored, as well as parts of the book they liked or connected with.

You may feel both nervous and excited at letting people see your story for the first time. That is totally normal! Just realise, whether someone likes your book (and I'm sure they will) or they don't care for it, it doesn't mean much. There are very well-written books, amazing books, that some people can't stand! It's impossible for even the best book to be liked by everyone.

One reason we use beta readers is because other people can often find problems with our stories that we can't see on our own. You know so much about your story, it is hard to step back and see it clearly and objectively.

You may know that your detective has a fear of hippos, but did you actually include that in the book? That zoo scene where the detective starts falling apart outside of the hippo tank won't make a whole lot of sense without that little piece of information. See? Beta readers can help you see things that you missed, and your story will be better off for it.

It can be especially hard to evaluate your own mystery all on your own. After all, you've known all along whodunnit! A beta reader can offer valuable insight into whether your mystery "works" or falls flat. You might ask them questions specific to your mystery. Did your clues work? Were they obvious, or were they hard to miss? Were there too many red herrings or not enough? Did they figure out whodunnit early on, or were they surprised at the end? Did they feel like your mystery made sense and was believable? These are all super important questions that only a beta reader can answer.

Understand that it can be hard to hear people say not-so-positive things about your precious story. It can be easy to take comments personally and feel like they're criticising you. You can even feel a little insulted. It's okay to just thank someone for their thoughts, whether you agree or not, and give yourself some space. Maybe write down what they said, and then forget about it for a little while. When you come back to it, I bet it won't affect you as much and you'll be in a better place to evaluate the comments they gave you.

Very important! You don't have to agree with or take every opinion you get about your story! Try not to dismiss people's thoughts—it's important to really hear what they are saying. But maybe they want you to change something that would really alter the heart of your story. You don't have to do that. Remember, this is *your* story. And opinions are like elbows. Everybody has one (or two). Some are helpful and some are not.

Once you get feedback from your beta readers and make any changes you want to make, you are done.

Do I need to say that again?

You can write those two beautiful, tiny words that every writer longs to write:

The End.

Conclusion

YOU'VE DONE IT—step by step, you've unravelled the mysteries of writing a captivating story. Let's take a moment to recap the journey you've embarked on.

You began by answering the essential questions: who's the villain, what's the crime, and why was it committed? These foundational elements laid the groundwork for your entire story. With a clear direction in mind, you then captured the essence of your narrative in a concise summary, providing yourself with a roadmap to follow as you wrote.

Next, you brought your characters to life, creating detailed profiles that gave them depth, backstories, and motivations, ensuring they would engage your readers and drive your plot forward. With your characters in place, you set the stage by choosing the perfect locations and settings to immerse your readers in the world you've created. You also made a crucial decision about who would tell the story, selecting the point of view that best fit your narrative style.

Armed with these key elements, you structured your story into acts, chapters, and scenes, carefully plotting the course your characters would take. You delved deep into the mind of your villain, mapping out their timeline to keep your hero—and your readers—on their toes. At the same time, you carefully planned your hero's journey, ensuring they would stay just one step behind the villain until it was time for the final showdown.

With the story structure in place, you became a master of misdirection, strategically burying clues and planting red herrings to keep your readers guessing until the very end. Then came the moment of truth, as you skillfully unraveled the mystery in a way that was both satisfying and surprising, tying together all the threads you'd woven throughout your story.

Finally, you took the time to write, revise, and refine your work, polishing your masterpiece until every word, sentence, and scene was just right. By following these steps, you've built a story that's more than just words on a page—it's an adventure waiting to be discovered by readers.

Now, it's time to share your mystery with the world. Whether this is your first book or one of many, you've developed skills that will serve you well in all your writing endeavours. So go ahead, crack open that notebook or fire up your computer—there are more mysteries to write, and you've got all the tools to solve them.

What are you waiting for?

Resources

Altair, Z. (2017, July 24). *Ten ways to hide clues in your mystery: surprise your reader*. The Thrill Begins. https://thrillbegins.com/2017/07/24/ten-ways-to-hide-clues-in-your-mystery-surprise-your-reader/

Altair, Z. (2020, September 16). *Whodunnit? Keep your reader guessing with red herrings, clues, and evidence*. ProWritingAid. https://prowritingaid.com/art/736/clues%2C-evidence%2C-and-red-herrings%3A-lead-your-reader-down-the-mystery.aspx

Azamber, T. (2016, April 15). *The significance of setting in mystery novels*. Terry Azamber. https://terryazamber.wordpress.com/2014/09/29/the-significance-of-setting-in-mystery-novels/

Biswas, P. M. (2021, March 3). *POV: choosing between first-person and third-person*. Writer's Digest. https://www.writersdigest.com/write-better-fiction/pov-choosing-between-first-person-and-third-person

Calvin, K. (2021, April 12). *Planting clues: red herrings that fool but don't frustrate your readers*. Writer's Digest. https://www.writersdigest.com/write-better-fiction/planting-clues-red-herrings-that-fool-but-dont-frustrate-your-readers

Curteman, N. (2011, December 11). *How to create minor characters in your mystery novel*. Global Mysteries. https://globalmysteriesblog.com/2010/08/09/how-to-create-minor-characters-in-your-mystery-novel/

Curteman, N. (2010, August 18). *9 Ways to create tension in a mystery novel*. Global Mysteries. https://globalmysteriesblog.com/2010/08/18/9-ways-to-create-tension-in-a-mystery-novel/

Hay, L. V. (2021, March 26). *How to organize a mystery novel*. WikiHow. https://www.wikihow.com/Organize-a-Mystery-Novel

Jain, S. (2021, October 8). *The science of storytelling explained: three-act structure!* BookWritten. https://bookwritten.com/the-science-of-storytelling-explained-three-act-structure/5335/

Jenkins, J. B. (2021, November 15). *What makes a great villain? Your checklist for writing a good bad guy*. Jerry Jenkins | Proven Writing Tips. https://jerryjenkins.com/what-makes-a-good-villain/

Jordan. (2021, October 21). *Writing a mystery novel: 7 items your story needs.* Now Novel. https://www.nownovel.com/blog/writing-a-mystery-novel/

Jordan. (2021, October 20). *Dramatic point of view: 5 tips for fly-on-the-wall scenes.* Now Novel. https://www.nownovel.com/blog/dramatic-point-of-view-tips/

Kaine, K. (2021, September 15). *A mystery novel template / cheatsheet / outline.* Novel Factory. https://www.novel-software.com/how-to-write-a-mystery-novel-outline/

Lambert, P. [Plottr]. (2021, January 24). *How to outline a mystery with the sleuth's journey (Free Plot Template)* [Video]. YouTube. https://www.youtube.com/watch?v=zCWjP2q1x-k&feature=youtu.be

McTaggart, F. (2020, November 3). *Using "Harry Potter" to understand "Save the Cat" novel structure.* MuggleNet. https://www.mugglenet.com/2020/11/using-harry-potter-to-understand-save-the-cat-novel-structure/

Poli, R. (2021, December 15). *12 Popular subgenres in mystery writing explained - the startup.* Medium. https://medium.com/swlh/12-popular-subgenres-in-mystery-writing-explained-d406a7248eed

Rogers, S. D. (2002). *Don't drop clues; place them carefully!* Writing-World.Com. https://www.writing-world.com/mystery/clues.shtml

Shoenberger, E. (2021, January 14). *Why locked room murder mysteries are the best.* BOOK RIOT. https://bookriot.com/what-are-locked-room-murder-mysteries/

Where does the expression "red herring" come from? (n.d.). Almanac.Com. Retrieved January 8, 2222, from https://www.almanac.com/fact/where-does-the-expression-red-herring-come

Index

If you found this book helpful,
I would be incredibly grateful if you took a few moments to leave a review on Amazon.
Thank you!

Ollie Ood

Other Books for Young Authors

Write a Novel

If you've enjoyed unraveling the mysteries of storytelling with this guide, why stop here? *How to Write a Novel Before You Turn 13* takes you beyond the twists and turns of a good mystery, offering 13 detailed steps to help young writers like you turn your creative ideas into a full-fledged novel.

Companion Workbook

Packed with prompts, exercises, and space to brainstorm, the companion workbook to *How to Write a Novel Before You Turn 13* is the perfect sidekick to your novel-writing journey. It's filled with activities that will guide you through each of the 13 steps, helping you develop characters, plot your story, and refine your ideas.

Books for All Authors

Craft Unforgettable Characters

Perfect for writers of all levels, this guide offers 10 customisable character templates and a list of 100 unique character quirks to add depth to your stories. Dive into character backstories, motivations, and more, with easy-to-follow steps.

Write Your Novel Here

Got a story idea but need a place to write it? *My Novel* is the perfect blank canvas, structured like a novel with a Title page, Table of Contents, and 120 lined pages. Plus, it includes four appendix worksheets to help you develop your storyline, plot points, and character profiles.

Ready to Take Your Mystery to the Next Level?

Dive deeper into your storytelling journey with our companion workbook! Packed with prompts, exercises, and guided activities, this workbook is designed to help you bring your ideas to life.

Whether you're planning characters, plotting twists, or fine-tuning your clues, this hands-on guide will walk you through each step of the process, giving you more tools to craft your mystery novel. Get ready to write, refine, and solve your story—one clue at a time!

Made in United States
Troutdale, OR
11/12/2024

24551704R00110